W9-AUJ-564

What Do You Expect?

Probability and Expected Value

Glenda Lappan, Elizabeth Difanis Phillips,
James T. Fey, Susan N. Friel

Pearson

Boston, Massachusetts

Connected Mathematics® was developed at Michigan State University with financial support from the Michigan State University Office of the Provost, Computing and Technology, and the College of Natural Science.

 This material is based upon work supported by the National Science Foundation under Grant No. MDR 9150217 and Grant No. ESI 9986372. Opinions expressed are those of the authors and not necessarily those of the Foundation.

As with prior editions of this work, the authors and administration of Michigan State University preserve a tradition of devoting royalties from this publication to support activities sponsored by the MSU Mathematics Education Enrichment Fund.

Acknowledgments appear on page 130, which constitutes an extension of this copyright page.

13-digit ISBN 978-0-328-90050-3
10-digit ISBN 0-328-90050-8
1 17

A Team of Experts

Glenda Lappan is a University Distinguished Professor in the Program in Mathematics Education (PRIME) and the Department of Mathematics at Michigan State University. Her research and development interests are in the connected areas of students' learning of mathematics and mathematics teachers' professional growth and change related to the development and enactment of K–12 curriculum materials.

Elizabeth Difanis Phillips is a Senior Academic Specialist in the Program in Mathematics Education (PRIME) and the Department of Mathematics at Michigan State University. She is interested in teaching and learning mathematics for both teachers and students. These interests have led to curriculum and professional development projects at the middle school and high school levels, as well as projects related to the teaching and learning of algebra across the grades.

James T. Fey is a Professor Emeritus at the University of Maryland. His consistent professional interest has been development and research focused on curriculum materials that engage middle and high school students in problem-based collaborative investigations of mathematical ideas and their applications.

Susan N. Friel is a Professor of Mathematics Education in the School of Education at the University of North Carolina at Chapel Hill. Her research interests focus on statistics education for middle-grade students and, more broadly, on teachers' professional development and growth in teaching mathematics K–8.

With... Yvonne Grant and Jacqueline Stewart

Yvonne Grant teaches mathematics at Portland Middle School in Portland, Michigan. Jacqueline Stewart is a recently retired high school teacher of mathematics at Okemos High School in Okemos, Michigan. Both Yvonne and Jacqueline have worked on a variety of activities related to the development, implementation, and professional development of the CMP curriculum since its beginning in 1991.

Development Team

CMP3 Authors

Glenda Lappan, University Distinguished Professor, Michigan State University
Elizabeth Difanis Phillips, Senior Academic Specialist, Michigan State University
James T. Fey, Professor Emeritus, University of Maryland
Susan N. Friel, Professor, University of North Carolina – Chapel Hill

With...

Yvonne Grant, Portland Middle School, Michigan
Jacqueline Stewart, Mathematics Consultant, Mason, Michigan

In Memory of... William M. Fitzgerald, Professor (Deceased), Michigan State University, who made substantial contributions to conceptualizing and creating CMP1.

Administrative Assistant

Michigan State University
Judith Martus Miller

Support Staff

Michigan State University
Undergraduate Assistants:
Bradley Robert Corlett, Carly Fleming, Erin Lucian, Scooter Nowak

Development Assistants

Michigan State University
Graduate Research Assistants:
Richard "Abe" Edwards, Nic Gilbertson, Funda Gonulates, Aladar Horvath, Eun Mi Kim, Kevin Lawrence, Jennifer Nimtz, Joanne Philhower, Sasha Wang

Assessment Team

Maine
Falmouth Public Schools
Falmouth Middle School: Shawn Towle

Michigan
Ann Arbor Public Schools
Tappan Middle School
Anne Marie Nicoll-Turner

Portland Public Schools
Portland Middle School
Holly DeRosia, Yvonne Grant

Traverse City Area Public Schools
Traverse City East Middle School
Jane Porath, Mary Beth Schmitt

Traverse City West Middle School
Jennifer Rundio, Karrie Tufts

Ohio
Clark-Shawnee Local Schools
Rockway Middle School: Jim Mamer

Content Consultants

Michigan State University
Peter Lappan, Professor Emeritus, Department of Mathematics

Normandale Community College
Christopher Danielson, Instructor, Department of Mathematics & Statistics

University of North Carolina – Wilmington
Dargan Frierson, Jr., Professor, Department of Mathematics & Statistics

Student Activities
Michigan State University
Brin Keller, Associate Professor, Department of Mathematics

Consultants

Indiana
Purdue University
Mary Bouck, Mathematics Consultant

Michigan
Oakland Schools
Valerie Mills, Mathematics Education
Supervisor
Mathematics Education Consultants:
Geraldine Devine, Dana Gosen

Ellen Bacon, Independent Mathematics
Consultant

New York
University of Rochester
Jeffrey Choppin, Associate Professor

Ohio
University of Toledo
Debra Johanning, Associate Professor

Pennsylvania
University of Pittsburgh
Margaret Smith, Professor

Texas
University of Texas at Austin
Emma Trevino, Supervisor of
Mathematics Programs, The Dana Center

Mathematics for All Consulting
Carmen Whitman, Mathematics Consultant

....

Reviewers

Michigan
Ionia Public Schools
Kathy Dole, Director of Curriculum
and Instruction

Grand Valley State University
Lisa Kasmer, Assistant Professor

Portland Public Schools
Teri Keusch, Classroom Teacher

Minnesota
Hopkins School District 270
Michele Luke, Mathematics Coordinator

....

Field Test Sites for CMP3

Michigan
Ann Arbor Public Schools
Tappan Middle School
Anne Marie Nicoll-Turner*

Portland Public Schools
Portland Middle School: Mark Braun,
Angela Buckland, Holly DeRosia,
Holly Feldpausch, Angela Foote,
Yvonne Grant*, Kristin Roberts,
Angie Stump, Tammi Wardwell

Traverse City Area Public Schools
Traverse City East Middle School
Ivanka Baic Berkshire, Brenda Dunscombe,
Tracie Herzberg, Deb Larimer, Jan Palkowski,
Rebecca Perreault, Jane Porath*,
Robert Sagan, Mary Beth Schmitt*

Traverse City West Middle School
Pamela Alfieri, Jennifer Rundio,
Maria Taplin, Karrie Tufts*

Maine
Falmouth Public Schools
Falmouth Middle School: Sally Bennett,
Chris Driscoll, Sara Jones, Shawn Towle*

Minnesota
Minneapolis Public Schools
Jefferson Community School
Leif Carlson*,
Katrina Hayek Munsisoumang*

Ohio
Clark-Shawnee Local Schools
Reid School: Joanne Gilley
Rockway Middle School: Jim Mamer*
Possum School: Tami Thomas

*Indicates a Field Test Site Coordinator

What Do You Expect?

Probability and Expected Value

Looking Ahead 2

Mathematical Highlights 4

Mathematical Practices and Habits of Mind 5

A First Look At Chance 7

1.1 Choosing Cereal Tossing a Coin to Find Probabilities 8

1.2 Tossing Paper Cups Finding More Probabilities 10

1.3 One More Try Finding Experimental Probabilities 12

1.4 Analyzing Events Understanding Equally Likely 15

ACE Homework 17

Mathematical Reflections 25

Experimental and Theoretical Probability 27

2.1 Predicting to Win Finding Theoretical Probabilities 28

2.2 Choosing Marbles Developing Probability Models 30

2.3 Designing a Fair Game Pondering Possible and Probable 32

2.4 Winning the Bonus Prize Using Strategies to Find
Theoretical Probabilities 34

ACE Homework 36

Mathematical Reflections 48

Making Decisions With Probability   50

3.1 Designing a Spinner to Find Probabilities 50

3.2 Making Decisions Analyzing Fairness 52

3.3 Roller Derby Analyzing a Game 54

3.4 Scratching Spots Designing and Using a Simulation 56

Ⓐ Ⓒ Ⓔ Homework 58

Mathematical Reflections 69

Analyzing Compound Events Using an Area Model   71

4.1 Drawing Area Models to Find the Sample Space 72

4.2 Making Purple Area Models and Probability 75

4.3 One-and-One Free Throws Simulating a Probability Situation 76

4.4 Finding Expected Value 78

Ⓐ Ⓒ Ⓔ Homework 80

Mathematical Reflections 97

Binomial Outcomes   99

5.1 Guessing Answers Finding More Expected Values 100

5.2 Ortonville Binomial Probability 101

5.3 A Baseball Series Expanding Binomial Probability 103

Ⓐ Ⓒ Ⓔ Homework 105

Mathematical Reflections 111

Unit Project The Carnival Game 113

Looking Back 115

English/Spanish Glossary 118

Index 127

Acknowledgments 130

Looking Ahead

For a game, each player guesses a color and chooses a block from a bucket. A player who correctly predicts the color wins. After each selection, the block is returned to the bucket. **What** are the chances of winning the game?

A scratch-off prize card has five spots. Two of the spots have a matching prize. You scratch off only two spots. If the prize under both spots match, you win. **How** likely is it that you will win?

Nishi is going to take a free throw. If she is successful, she is allowed to attempt a second free throw. **How** can you determine whether Nishi is most likely to score 0, 1, or 2 points?

Probabilities can help you make decisions. If there is a 75% chance of rain, you might decide to carry an umbrella. If a baseball player has a 0.245 batting average, you expect that he is more likely not to get a hit than to get a hit on a given at-bat.

Probabilities can also help you to predict what will happen over the long run. Suppose you and a friend toss a coin before each bus ride to decide who will sit by the window. You can predict that you will sit by the window about half of the time.

Many probability situations involve a payoff—points scored in a game, lives saved by promoting good health, or profit earned from a business venture. You can sometimes find the long-term average payoff. For example, when deciding whether to make an investment, a company might figure out how much it can expect to earn over the long run.

In this Unit, you will look at questions involving probability and expected value, including the three questions on the opposite page.

Mathematical Highlights

What Do You Expect?

In this Unit, you will deepen your understanding of basic probability concepts. You will learn about the expected value of situations involving chance.

You will learn how to

- Use probabilities to predict what will happen over the long run

- Distinguish between equally likely events and those that are not equally likely

- Use strategies for identifying possible outcomes and analyzing probabilities, such as using lists or tree diagrams

- Develop two kinds of probability models:

  (1) Gather data from experiments (experimental probability)

  (2) Analyze possible outcomes (theoretical probability)

- Understand that experimental probabilities are better estimates of theoretical probabilities when they are based on larger numbers of trials

- Determine if a game is fair or unfair

- Use models to analyze situations that involve two stages (or actions)

- Determine the expected value of a chance situation

- Analyze situations that involve binomial outcomes

- Interpret statements of probability to make decisions and answer questions

As you work on Problems in this Unit, ask yourself questions about situations that involve analyzing probabilities:

What are the possible outcomes for the event(s) in this situation?

Are these outcomes equally likely?

Is this a fair or unfair situation?

Can I compute the theoretical probabilities or do I conduct an experiment?

How can I determine the probability of one event followed by a second event: two-stage probabilities?

How can I use expected value to help me make decisions?

Mathematical Practices and Habits of Mind

In the *Connected Mathematics* curriculum you will develop an understanding of important mathematical ideas by solving problems and reflecting on the mathematics involved. Every day, you will use "habits of mind" to make sense of problems and apply what you learn to new situations. Some of these habits are described by the *Common Core State Standards for Mathematical Practices* (MP).

MP1 Make sense of problems and persevere in solving them.

When using mathematics to solve a problem, it helps to think carefully about

- data and other facts you are given and what additional information you need to solve the problem;
- strategies you have used to solve similar problems and whether you could solve a related simpler problem first;
- how you could express the problem with equations, diagrams, or graphs;
- whether your answer makes sense.

MP2 Reason abstractly and quantitatively.

When you are asked to solve a problem, it often helps to

- focus first on the key mathematical ideas;
- check that your answer makes sense in the problem setting;
- use what you know about the problem setting to guide your mathematical reasoning.

MP3 Construct viable arguments and critique the reasoning of others.

When you are asked to explain why a conjecture is correct, you can

- show some examples that fit the claim and explain why they fit;
- show how a new result follows logically from known facts and principles.

When you believe a mathematical claim is incorrect, you can

- show one or more counterexamples—cases that don't fit the claim;
- find steps in the argument that do not follow logically from prior claims.

MP4 Model with mathematics.

When you are asked to solve problems, it often helps to

- think carefully about the numbers or geometric shapes that are the most important factors in the problem, then ask yourself how those factors are related to each other;
- express data and relationships in the problem with tables, graphs, diagrams, or equations, and check your result to see if it makes sense.

MP5 Use appropriate tools strategically.

When working on mathematical questions, you should always

- decide which tools are most helpful for solving the problem and why;
- try a different tool when you get stuck.

MP6 Attend to precision.

In every mathematical exploration or problem-solving task, it is important to

- think carefully about the required accuracy of results; is a number estimate or geometric sketch good enough, or is a precise value or drawing needed?
- report your discoveries with clear and correct mathematical language that can be understood by those to whom you are speaking or writing.

MP7 Look for and make use of structure.

In mathematical explorations and problem solving, it is often helpful to

- look for patterns that show how data points, numbers, or geometric shapes are related to each other;
- use patterns to make predictions.

MP8 Look for and express regularity in repeated reasoning.

When results of a repeated calculation show a pattern, it helps to

- express that pattern as a general rule that can be used in similar cases;
- look for shortcuts that will make the calculation simpler in other cases.

You will use all of the Mathematical Practices in this Unit. Sometimes, when you look at a Problem, it is obvious which practice is most helpful. At other times, you will decide on a practice to use during class explorations and discussions. After completing each Problem, ask yourself:

- What mathematics have I learned by solving this Problem?
- What Mathematical Practices were helpful in learning this mathematics?

A First Look At Chance

Decisions, decisions, decisions—you make decisions every day. You choose what to wear, with whom to have lunch, what to do after school, and maybe what time to go to bed.

To make some decisions, you consider the chance, or likelihood, that something will happen. You may listen to the weather forecast to decide whether you will wear a raincoat to school. In some cases, you may even let chance make a decision for you, such as when you roll a number cube to see who goes first in a game.

A number cube shows the numbers 1, 2, 3, 4, 5, and 6 on its faces.

Common Core State Standards

7.SP.C.6 Approximate the probability of a chance event by collecting data on the chance process that produces it and observing its long-run relative frequency, and predict the approximate relative frequency given the probability.

7.SP.C.7a Develop a uniform probability model by assigning equal probability to all outcomes, and use the model to determine probabilities of events.

7.SP.C.7b Develop a probability model (which may not be uniform) by observing frequencies in data generated from a chance process.

Also 7.RP.A.2, 7.SP.C.8, 7.SP.C.8a, 7.SP.C.8b

Think about these questions. They are examples of probability situations to help you consider the likelihood of particular events.

- What are the chances of getting a 2 when you roll a number cube? Are you more likely to roll a 2 or a 6? How can you decide?

- The weather forecaster says the chance of rain tomorrow is 40%. What does this mean? Should you wear a raincoat?

- When you toss a coin, what are the chances of getting tails?

- Suppose you toss seven tails in a row. Are you more likely to get heads or tails on the next toss?

1.1 Choosing Cereal
Tossing Coins to Find Probabilities

Kalvin always has cereal for breakfast. He likes Cocoa Blast cereal, but his mother wants him to eat Health Nut Flakes at least some mornings.

Kalvin and his mother agree to leave the cereal problem to chance. Each morning in June, Kalvin tosses a coin. If the coin lands on heads, he will have Cocoa Blast. If the coin lands on tails, he will have Health Nut Flakes.

? Predict how many days Kalvin can expect to eat Cocoa Blast in June.

Problem 1.1

A 1. Test your prediction. Toss a coin 30 times (one for each day in June). Record your results in a table with the headings below. Your table will have 30 rows.

Coin-Toss Results

Day	Result of Toss (H or T)	Number of Heads So Far	Fraction of Heads So Far	Percent of Heads So Far
1	■	■	■	■
2	■	■	■	■

2. As you add more data, what happens to the percent of tosses that are heads?

B Work with your classmates to combine the results from all the groups.

1. What percent of the total number of tosses for your class is heads?

2. As your class adds more data, what happens to the percent of tosses that are heads?

3. Based on what you found for June, how many times do you expect Kalvin to eat Cocoa Blast in July? Explain your reasoning.

C Kalvin's mother tells him that the chance of a coin showing heads when he tosses it is $\frac{1}{2}$. Does this mean that every time he tosses a coin twice, he will get one head and one tail? Explain.

ACE Homework starts on page 17.

1.2 Tossing Paper Cups
Finding More Probabilities

Kalvin wants to find something else to toss that will give him a better chance of eating his favorite cereal each morning. He wonders if a paper cup would be a good thing to toss.

Because Kalvin wants to eat Cocoa Blast cereal more of the time, he needs to determine if the cup lands in one position more often than another. If so, he will ask to toss a paper cup instead of a coin.

End   Side   End   Side   End

? Kalvin wants the best chance of eating Cocoa Blast. Which of the landing positions, end or side, should Kalvin use to represent Cocoa Blast? Explain your answer.

Problem 1.2

A Conduct an experiment to test your prediction about how a paper cup lands. Toss a paper cup 50 times. Make a table to record your data.

B Use your results to answer the following questions:

1. For what fraction of your 50 tosses did the cup land on one of its ends? What percent is this?

2. For what fraction of your 50 tosses did the cup land on its side? What percent is this?

3. Do the landing positions *end* and *side* have the same chance of occurring? If not, which is more likely? Explain.

4. Which of the cup's landing positions should Kalvin use to represent Cocoa Blast? Explain your reasoning.

C Combine the data from all the groups in your class. Based on these data, would you change your answers to parts (3) and (4) of Question B? Explain.

D Kalvin's mother agrees to let him use a cup to decide his cereal each morning. On the first morning, the cup lands on its end. On the second morning, it lands on its side. Kalvin says, "This cup isn't any better than the coin. It lands on an end 50% of the time!" Do you agree or disagree with Kalvin? Explain.

A C E Homework starts on page 17.

1.3 One More Try
Finding Experimental Probabilities

In the last two Problems, you conducted experiments to find the chances of particular results. You represented those chances as fractions or percents. The mathematical word for chance is **probability.** A probability that you find by conducting an experiment and collecting data is called an **experimental probability.**

Suppose you toss a paper cup 50 times, and it lands on its side 31 times. Each toss of the cup is a **trial.** In this experiment, there are 50 trials. **Favorable outcomes** are the trials in which a desired result occurs.

In this case, a favorable result, *landed on side,* occurred 31 times. To find the experimental probability, use the ratio below.

$$\frac{\text{number of favorable outcomes}}{\text{total number of trials}}$$

You can write "the probability of the cup landing on its side" as $P(\text{side})$. The equation below gives the results of the experiment just described.

$$P(\text{side}) = \frac{\text{number of times cup landed on its side}}{\text{number of times cup was tossed}} = \frac{31}{50}$$

The ratio of number of desired results to the total number of trials is also called **relative frequency.**

Kalvin has come up with one more way to use probability to decide his breakfast cereal. This time, he tosses two coins.

- If the coins match, he gets to eat Cocoa Blast.

Match

Match

- If the coins do not match, he eats Health Nut Flakes.

No Match

? Suppose Kalvin's mother agrees to let him use this method. How many days in June do you think Kalvin will eat Cocoa Blast?

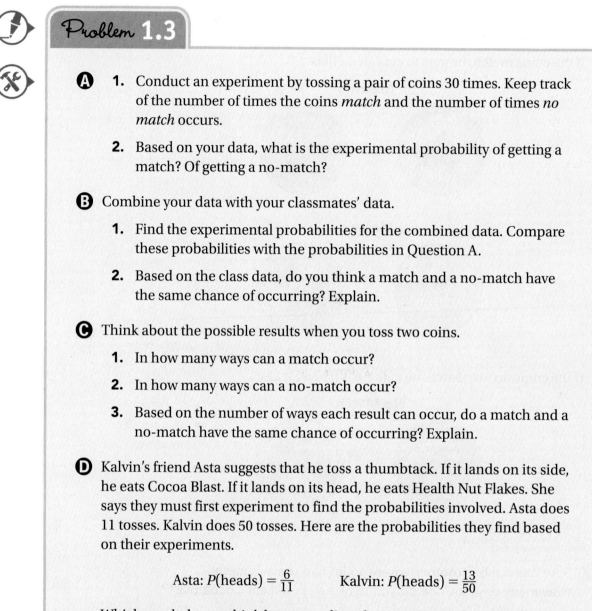

Problem 1.3

A **1.** Conduct an experiment by tossing a pair of coins 30 times. Keep track of the number of times the coins *match* and the number of times *no match* occurs.

2. Based on your data, what is the experimental probability of getting a match? Of getting a no-match?

B Combine your data with your classmates' data.

1. Find the experimental probabilities for the combined data. Compare these probabilities with the probabilities in Question A.

2. Based on the class data, do you think a match and a no-match have the same chance of occurring? Explain.

C Think about the possible results when you toss two coins.

1. In how many ways can a match occur?

2. In how many ways can a no-match occur?

3. Based on the number of ways each result can occur, do a match and a no-match have the same chance of occurring? Explain.

D Kalvin's friend Asta suggests that he toss a thumbtack. If it lands on its side, he eats Cocoa Blast. If it lands on its head, he eats Health Nut Flakes. She says they must first experiment to find the probabilities involved. Asta does 11 tosses. Kalvin does 50 tosses. Here are the probabilities they find based on their experiments.

$$\text{Asta: } P(\text{heads}) = \frac{6}{11} \qquad \text{Kalvin: } P(\text{heads}) = \frac{13}{50}$$

Which result do you think better predicts the experimental probability of the thumbtack landing on its head when tossed? Explain.

A C E Homework starts on page 17.

1.4 Analyzing Events
Understanding *Equally Likely*

Kalvin finds a coin near a railroad track. It looks flat and a little bent, so he guesses it has been run over by a train. He decides to use this unusual coin to choose his breakfast cereal during November. By the end of the month, he has had Health Nut Flakes only seven times. His mother is suspicious of the coin.

- Why is Kalvin's mother suspicious of the coin?

- What does it mean for a coin to be "fair"?

She says, "You call a coin a fair coin if heads and tails are **equally likely** results of a coin toss." This means that you have the same chance of getting heads as getting tails. Kalvin and his mother wonder if Kalvin's coin is a fair coin.

Kalvin's mother says, "Suppose each person in our family writes his or her name on a card and puts the card in a hat. If you mix up the three cards and pull one out, all three names are equally likely to be picked. But suppose I put my name in the hat ten times. Then the names are not equally likely to be picked. My name has a greater chance of being chosen."

- Why is each card equally likely to be chosen, but each name is not?

- Kalvin and his father want all three names equally likely to be chosen. How many cards should they add to the hat so that each name is equally likely to be chosen? What should be on each card?

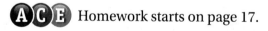

Problem 1.4

A The list below gives several actions and possible results. In each case, decide whether the possible results are equally likely and explain. For actions 5 and 6, start by listing all the possible results.

Action	**Possible Results**
1. You toss an empty juice can.	The can lands on its side, the can lands upside-down, or the can lands right-side-up.
2. A baby is born.	The baby is a boy or the baby is a girl.
3. A baby is born.	The baby is right-handed or the baby is left-handed.
4. A high school team plays a football game.	The team wins or the team loses.
5. You roll a six-sided number cube.	_____
6. You guess an answer on a true-or-false test.	_____

B For which of the actions in Question A did you find the results to be equally likely? Does this mean that the probability of each result is $\frac{1}{2}$ (or 50%)? Explain your reasoning.

C Describe an action for which the results are equally likely. Then, describe an action for which the results are *not* equally likely.

ACE Homework starts on page 17.

Applications

1. **a.** Miki tosses a coin 50 times, and the coin shows heads 28 times. What fraction of the 50 tosses is heads? What percent is this?

   b. Suppose the coin is fair, and Miki tosses it 500 times. About how many times can she expect it to show heads? Explain your reasoning.

2. Suppose Kalvin tosses a coin to determine his breakfast cereal every day. He starts on his twelfth birthday and continues until his eighteenth birthday. About how many times would you expect him to eat Cocoa Blast cereal?

3. Kalvin tosses a coin five days in a row and gets tails every time. Do you think there is something wrong with the coin? How can you find out?

4. Len tosses a coin three times. The coin shows heads every time. What are the chances the coin shows tails on the next toss? Explain.

5. Is it possible to toss a coin 20 times and have it land heads-up 20 times? Is this likely to happen? Explain.

6. Kalvin tosses a paper cup once each day for a year to determine his breakfast cereal. Use your results from Problem 1.2 to answer the following.

   a. How many times do you expect the cup to land on its side? On one of its ends?

   b. How many times do you expect Kalvin to eat Cocoa Blast in a month? In a year? Explain.

7. Dawn tosses a pawn from her chess set five times. It lands on its base four times and on its side only once.

   Andre tosses the same pawn 100 times. It lands on its base 28 times and on its side 72 times. Based on their data, if you toss the pawn one more time, is it more likely to land on its base or its side? Explain.

8. Kalvin flips a small paper cup 50 times and a large paper cup 30 times. The table below displays the results of his experiments. Based on these data, should he use the small cup or the large cup to determine his breakfast each morning? Explain.

Cup-Toss Results

Where Cup Lands	Small Paper Cup	Large Paper Cup
Side	39 times	22 times
One of Its Ends	11 times	8 times

9. Kalvin's sister Kate finds yet another way for him to pick his breakfast. She places one blue marble and one red marble in each of two bags. She says that each morning he can choose one marble from each bag. If the marbles are the same color, he eats Cocoa Blast. If not, he eats Health Nut Flakes. Explain how selecting one marble from each of the two bags and tossing two coins are similar.

10. Adsila and Adahy have to decide who will take out the garbage. Adahy suggests they toss two coins. He says that if at least one head comes up, Adsila takes out the garbage. If no heads come up, Adahy takes out the garbage. Should Adsila agree to Adahy's proposal? Explain why or why not.

For Exercises 11–15, decide whether the possible results are equally likely. Explain.

Action

Possible Results

11. Your phone rings at 9:00 P.M.

The caller is your best friend, the caller is a relative, or the caller is someone else.

12. You check the temperature at your home tomorrow morning.

The temperature is 30°F or above, or the temperature is below 30°F.

13. You spin the pointer once.

The pointer lands on yellow, the pointer lands on red, or the pointer lands on blue.

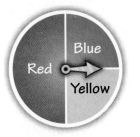

14. You find out how many car accidents occurred in your city or town yesterday.

There were fewer than five accidents, there were exactly five accidents, or there were more than five accidents.

15. You choose a card from a standard deck of playing cards (with no jokers).

The card is a spade, the card is a heart, the card is a diamond, or the card is a club.

For Exercises 16–17, first list all the possible results for each action. Then decide whether the results are equally likely.

16. You choose a block from a bag containing one red block, three blue blocks, and one green block.

17. You try to steal second base during a baseball game.

18. For parts (a)–(f), give an example of a result that would have a probability near the percent given.

    a. 0%　　　　　**b.** 25%　　　　　**c.** 50%

    d. 75%　　　　　**e.** 80%　　　　　**f.** 100%

Connections

19. Colby rolls a number cube 50 times. She records the result of each roll and organizes her data in the table below.

Number Cube Results

Number	Frequency
1	~~||||~~	
2	~~||||~~ ||||
3	~~||||~~	
4	~~||||~~ |||
5	~~||||~~ ~~||||~~	
6	~~||||~~ ~~||||~~

a. What fraction of the rolls are 2's? What percent is this?

b. What fraction of the rolls are odd numbers? What percent is this?

c. What percent of the rolls is greater than 3?

d. Suppose Colby rolls the number cube 100 times. About how many times can she expect to roll a 2? Explain.

e. If Colby rolls the number cube 1,000 times, about how many times can she expect to roll an odd number? Explain.

20. Find a fraction between each pair of fractions.

a. $\frac{1}{10}$ and $\frac{8}{25}$

b. $\frac{3}{8}$ and $\frac{11}{40}$

For Exercises 21–23, use the bar graph below.

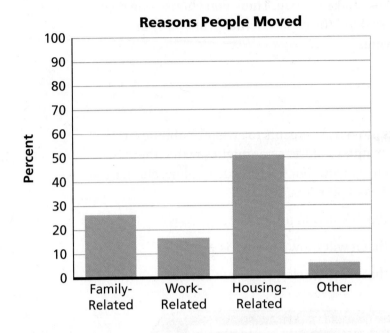

Reasons People Moved

21. **Multiple Choice** Suppose 41,642 people moved. About how many of those people moved for family-related reasons?

    A. 28   **B.** 11,000   **C.** 21,000   **D.** 31,000

22. **Multiple Choice** What fraction of the people represented in the graph moved for reasons other than work-related, housing-related, or family-related?

    F. $\frac{6}{10}$ **G.** $\frac{6}{100}$ **H.** $\frac{52}{100}$ **J.** $\frac{94}{100}$

23. **Multiple Choice** Suppose 41,642 people moved. About how many moved for housing-related reasons?

    A. 52   **B.** 11,000   **C.** 21,000   **D.** 31,000

24. Suppose you write all the factors of 42 on pieces of paper and put them in a bag. You shake the bag. Then, you choose one piece of paper from the bag. Find the experimental probability of choosing the following.

   a. an even number

   b. a prime number

25. Weather forecasters often use percents to give probabilities in their forecasts. For example, a forecaster might say that there is a 50% chance of rain tomorrow. For the forecasts below, change the fractional probabilities to percents.

   a. The probability that it will rain tomorrow is $\frac{2}{5}$.

   b. The probability that it will snow Monday is $\frac{3}{10}$.

   c. The probability that it will be cloudy this weekend is $\frac{3}{5}$.

For Exercises 26–29, use the graph below.

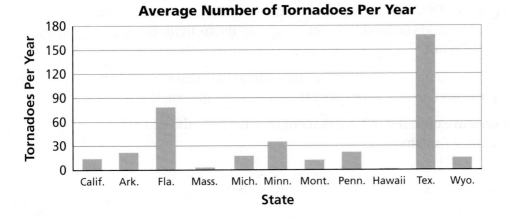

Average Number of Tornadoes Per Year

26. Is a tornado equally likely to occur in California and in Florida? Explain your reasoning.

27. Is a tornado equally likely to occur in Arkansas and in Pennsylvania?

28. Is a tornado equally likely to occur in Massachusetts and in Texas?

29. Based on these data, is a person living in Montana more likely to experience a tornado than a person living in Massachusetts? Explain.

Extensions

30. Monday is the first day Kalvin tosses a coin to determine his cereal. During the first five days, he has Cocoa Blast only twice. One possible pattern of Kalvin's coin tosses is shown.

Coin-Toss Results

Monday	Tuesday	Wednesday	Thursday	Friday
H	H	T	T	T

Find every way Kalvin can toss the coin during the week and have Cocoa Blast cereal twice. Explain how you know that you found every possible way.

31. Yolanda watches a carnival game in which a paper cup is tossed. It costs $1 to play the game. If the cup lands upright, the player receives $5. Otherwise, the player receives nothing. The cup is tossed 50 times. It lands on its side 32 times, upside-down 13 times, and upright 5 times.

    a. If Yolanda plays the game ten times, about how many times can she expect to win? How many times can she expect to lose?

    b. Do you expect her to have more or less money at the end of ten games? Explain.

Mathematical Reflections

In this Investigation, you conducted experiments with coins and paper cups. You used fractions and percents to express the chances, or probabilities, that certain results would occur. You also considered several actions and determined whether the possible results were equally likely. The questions below will help you summarize what you have learned.

Think about these questions. Discuss your ideas with other students and your teacher. Then write a summary of your findings in your notebook.

1. **How** do you find the experimental probability that a particular result will occur? **Why** is it called the experimental probability?

2. In an experiment, are 30 trials as good as 500 trials to predict the chances of a result? **Explain**.

3. **What** does it mean for results to be equally likely?

Common Core Mathematical Practices

As you worked on the Problems in this Investigation, you used prior knowledge to make sense of them. You also applied Mathematical Practices to solve the Problems. Think back over your work, the ways you thought about the Problems, and how you used Mathematical Practices.

Hector described his thoughts in the following way:

> Our group noticed that in Problem 1.2, Kalvin tries another method for choosing his cereal. He flips a cup and records how the cup lands, on either an end or a side.
>
> At first we thought that the results would be the same as those for tossing a coin. After we tossed the cup 50 times, we were not so sure. It landed on its side 27 times and on its end 23 times.
>
> After we combined the class data, we were fairly certain that the two events were not equally likely. The cup would land on its side more often than on its end.

Common Core Standards for Mathematical Practice

MP7 Look for and make use of structure.

?
- What other Mathematical Practices can you identify in Hector's reasoning?

- Describe a Mathematical Practice that you and your classmates used to solve a different Problem in this Investigation.

Experimental and Theoretical Probability

In the last Investigation, you collected the results of many coin tosses. You found that the experimental probability of a coin landing on heads is $\frac{1}{2}$ $\left(\text{or very close to } \frac{1}{2}\right)$.

You assume that the coins are fair coins for which there are two equally likely results of a toss, heads or tails. The word **outcome** means an individual result of an action or event.

The coin-tossing experiment had two possible outcomes, heads and tails. Heads was a favorable outcome for Kalvin. A probability calculated by examining possible outcomes, rather than by experimenting, is a **theoretical probability.**

$$P(\text{heads}) = \frac{\text{number of ways heads can occur}}{\text{number of outcomes}} = \frac{1}{2}$$

The probability of tossing heads is 1 of 2, or $\frac{1}{2}$. The probability of tossing tails is also $\frac{1}{2}$.

Common Core State Standards

7.SP.C.5 Understand that the probability of a chance event is a number between 0 and 1 that expresses the likelihood of the event occurring.

7.SP.C. 8 Find probabilities of compound events using organized lists, tables, tree diagrams, and simulation.

7.SP.C.8c Design and use a simulation to generate frequencies for compound events.

Also 7.RP.A.2, 7.RP.A.2a, 7.RP.A.3, 7.SP.C.6, 7.SP.C.7b, 7.SP.C.8b, 7.SP.C.8a

But all experiments do not result in equally likely outcomes. When you tossed a cup, the two outcomes were not equally likely. The chances of landing on the side and landing in an upright position were not the same.

In this Investigation, you will explore some other situations in which probabilities are found both by experimenting and by analyzing the possible outcomes.

2.1 Predicting to Win
Finding Theoretical Probabilities

In the last 5 minutes of the *Gee Whiz Everyone Wins!* game show, all the members of the audience are called to the stage. Each one chooses a block *at random* from a bucket containing an unknown number of red, yellow, and blue blocks. Each block has the same size and shape.

Before choosing, each contestant predicts the color of his or her block. If the prediction is correct, the contestant wins. After each selection, the block is put back into the bucket and the bucket is shaken. That way, the probabilities do not change as blocks are removed.

- What do you think *random* means?

- Suppose you are a member of the audience. Would you rather be called to the stage first or last? Explain.

- Does it matter that the block is returned to the bucket and the bucket is shaken after each contestant? Explain.

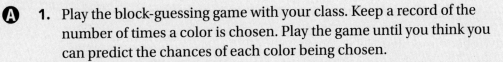

Problem 2.1

A 1. Play the block-guessing game with your class. Keep a record of the number of times a color is chosen. Play the game until you think you can predict the chances of each color being chosen.

2. Based on the data you collect during the game, find the experimental probabilities of choosing red, choosing yellow, and choosing blue.

B 1. Suppose you counted the red blocks, the blue blocks, and the yellow blocks in the bucket. How would you use this information to calculate the theoretical probability of drawing a red, a blue, or a yellow block?

2. How do the theoretical probabilities compare to the experimental probabilities in Question A?

3. What is the sum of the theoretical probabilities in Question B part (1)?

C 1. Does each individual block, without regard to color, have the same chance of being chosen? Explain.

2. Does each color have the same chance of being chosen? Explain.

3. If you choose a block, is it equally likely that it will be red or blue?

4. Which person has the advantage—the first person to choose from the bucket or the last person? Explain.

D Suppose you have a different bucket. You can't see inside, but you know there are 30 blocks in all. How can you use your observations of others picking blocks to predict how many of each color there are?

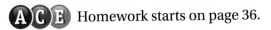 Homework starts on page 36.

2.2 Choosing Marbles
Developing Probability Models

Sammy collects marbles. He asks his teacher if the class could experiment with marbles instead of blocks. The teacher says, "What really matters is whether we can predict the probabilities in a situation using marbles. Let's try a bag with marbles of different colors."

Problem 2.2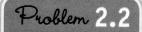

A A bag contains two yellow **marbles**, four blue marbles, and six red marbles. You choose a marble from **the bag** at random. Answer the following questions and explain your reasoning.

1. What is the probability the marble is yellow? The probability it is blue? The probability it is red?

2. What is the sum of the probabilities from part (1)?

3. What color is the selected marble most likely to be?

4. What is the probability the marble is not blue?

5. What is the probability the marble is either red or yellow?

6. What is the probability the marble is white?

7. Jakayla says the probability the marble is blue is $\frac{12}{4}$. Adsila says $\frac{12}{4}$ is impossible. Which girl is correct?

Problem 2.2 *continued*

B Suppose a new bag has twice as many marbles of each color.

    1. Do the probabilities change? Explain.

    2. How many blue marbles should you add to this bag to have the probability of choosing a blue marble equal to $\frac{1}{2}$?

C A different bag contains several marbles. Each marble is red or white or blue. The probability of choosing a red marble is $\frac{1}{3}$, and the probability of choosing a white marble is $\frac{1}{6}$.

    1. What is the probability of choosing a blue marble? Explain.

    2. What is the least number of marbles that can be in the bag? Suppose the bag contains the least number of marbles. How many of each color does the bag contain?

    3. Can the bag contain 48 marbles? If so, how many of each color does it contain?

    4. Suppose the bag contains 8 red marbles and 4 white marbles. How many blue marbles does it contain?

D **1.** Do you think the experimental probabilities would be different with blocks instead of marbles? How about theoretical probabilities?

    2. Design a fair way for Kalvin to choose his breakfast cereal using blocks or marbles.

A C E Homework starts on page 36.

2.3 Designing a Fair Game
Pondering Possible and Probable

Santo and Tevy are playing a game with coins. They take turns tossing three coins. If all three coins match, Santo wins. Otherwise, Tevy wins. Each player has won several turns in the game. Tevy, however, seems to be winning more often. Santo thinks the game is unfair. A **fair game** is a game in which all players have equal chances of winning.

Santo drew the tree diagram below to represent tossing three coins. A **tree diagram** is an illustration using branches to show the sample space of an event. The **sample space** is another name for the set of possible outcomes of an event.

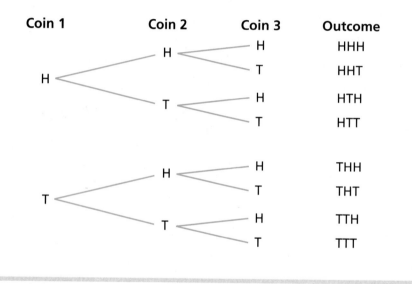

Coin 1	Coin 2	Coin 3	Outcome
H	H	H	HHH
		T	HHT
	T	H	HTH
		T	HTT
T	H	H	THH
		T	THT
	T	H	TTH
		T	TTT

? How can you decide if a game is fair or not?

Problem 2.3

A Use the tree diagram from above to answer the following questions:

   1. What is the sample space for tossing three coins?

   2. How many possible outcomes are there when you toss three coins? Are the outcomes equally likely?

   3. What is the theoretical probability that the three coins will match?

   4. What is the theoretical probability that exactly two coins will match?

   5. Is the game played by Santo and Tevy a fair game? If so, explain why. If not, explain how to make it fair.

B Suppose you tossed three coins for 24 trials. How many times would you expect two coins to match?

C Santo said, "It is *possible* to toss three coins and have them match." Tevy replied, "Yes, but is it *probable*?" What do you think each boy meant?

 Homework starts on page 36.

2.4 Winning the Bonus Prize
Using Strategies to Find Theoretical Probabilities

All the winners from the *Gee Whiz Everyone Wins!* game show have the opportunity to compete for a bonus prize. Each winner chooses one block from each of two bags. Each bag contains one red, one yellow, and one blue block. This bonus game consists of two events, which can also be called a **compound event.**

The contestant must predict which color she or he will choose from each of the two bags. If the prediction is correct, the contestant wins a $10,000 bonus prize!

- What color choice gives you the best chance of winning?

Problem 2.4

(A) 1. Conduct an experiment with 36 trials for the situation above. Record the pairs of colors that you choose.

2. Find the experimental probability of choosing each possible pair of colors.

(B) 1. Find all of the possible color pairs that can be chosen. Are these outcomes equally likely? Explain your reasoning.

2. Find the theoretical probability of choosing each pair of colors.

3. How do the theoretical probabilities compare with your experimental probabilities? Explain any differences.

(C) 1. Brelynn and Akimi change the rules of the game. Each contestant must predict which color combination will result from choosing a block from each bag. Brelynn and Akimi make the following predictions for this game.

> Akimi: I predict 2 reds.
>
> Brelynn: I predict 1 blue and 1 red, in either order.

Who has the better chance of winning? Explain.

2. Does a contestant have a chance to win the bonus prize? Is it likely a contestant will win the bonus prize? Explain.

3. If you play this game 18 times, how many times do you expect to win?

 Homework starts on page 36.

Applications

1. A bucket contains one green block, one red block, and two yellow blocks. You choose one block from the bucket.

   a. Find the theoretical probability that you will choose each color.

   $P(\text{green}) = $ ■ $P(\text{yellow}) = $ ■ $P(\text{red}) = $ ■

   b. Find the sum of the probabilities in part (a).

   c. What is the probability that you will *not* choose a red block? Explain how you found your answer.

   d. What is the sum of the probability of choosing a red block and the probability of not choosing a red block?

2. A bubble-gum machine contains 25 gumballs. There are 12 green, 6 purple, 2 orange, and 5 yellow gumballs.

   a. Find each theoretical probability.

   $P(\text{green}) = $ ■ $P(\text{purple}) = $ ■

   $P(\text{orange}) = $ ■ $P(\text{yellow}) = $ ■

   b. Find the sum.

   $P(\text{green}) + P(\text{purple}) + P(\text{orange}) + P(\text{yellow}) = $ ■

   c. Write each of the probabilities in part (a) as a percent.

   $P(\text{green}) = $ ■ $P(\text{purple}) = $ ■

   $P(\text{orange}) = $ ■ $P(\text{yellow}) = $ ■

   d. What is the sum of all the probabilities as a percent?

   e. What do you think the sum of the probabilities for all the possible outcomes must be for any situation? Explain.

3. Bailey uses the results from an experiment to calculate the probability of each color of block being chosen from a bucket. He says $P(\text{red}) = 35\%$, $P(\text{blue}) = 45\%$, and $P(\text{yellow}) = 20\%$. Jarod uses theoretical probability because he knows how many of each color block is in the bucket. He says $P(\text{red}) = 45\%$, $P(\text{blue}) = 35\%$, and $P(\text{yellow}) = 20\%$. On Bailey's turn, he predicts blue. On Jarod's turn, he predicts red. Neither boy makes the right prediction.

   a. Did the boys make reasonable predictions based on their own probabilities? Explain.

   b. Did they do something wrong with their calculations? Explain.

4. A bag contains two white blocks, one red block, and three purple blocks. You choose one block from the bag.

   a. Find each probability.

   $P(\text{white}) = $ ■ $P(\text{red}) = $ ■ $P(\text{purple}) = $ ■

   b. What is the probability of *not* choosing a white block? Explain how you found your answer.

   c. Suppose the number of blocks of each color is doubled. What happens to the probability of choosing each color?

   d. Suppose you add two more blocks of each color to the original bag. What happens to the probability of choosing each color?

   e. How many blocks of which colors should you add to the original bag to make the probability of choosing a red block equal to $\frac{1}{2}$?

5. A bag contains exactly three blue blocks. You choose a block at random. Find each probability.

   a. $P(\text{blue})$

   b. $P(not \text{ blue})$

   c. $P(\text{yellow})$

6. A bag contains several marbles. Some are red, some are white, and some are blue. You count the marbles and find the theoretical probability of choosing a red marble is $\frac{1}{5}$. You also find the theoretical probability of choosing a white marble is $\frac{3}{10}$.

a. What is the least number of marbles that can be in the bag?

b. Can the bag contain 60 marbles? If so, how many of each color does it contain?

c. If the bag contains 4 red marbles and 6 white marbles, how many blue marbles does it contain?

d. How can you find the probability of choosing a blue marble?

7. Decide whether each statement is *true* or *false*. Justify your answers.

a. The probability of an outcome can be 0.

b. The probability of an outcome can be 1.

c. The probability of an outcome can be greater than 1.

8. Patricia and Jean design a coin-tossing game. Patricia suggests tossing three coins. Jean says they can toss one coin three times. Are the outcomes different for the two situations? Explain.

9. Pietro and Eva are playing a game in which they toss a coin three times. Eva gets a point if no two consecutive toss results match (as in H-T-H). Pietro gets a point if exactly two consecutive toss results match (as in H-H-T). If all three toss results match, no one scores a point. The first player to get 10 points wins. Is this a fair game? Explain. If it is not a fair game, change the rules to make it fair.

10. Silvia and Juanita are designing a game. A player in the game tosses two number cubes. Winning depends on whether the sum of the two numbers is odd or even. Silvia and Juanita make a tree diagram of possible outcomes.

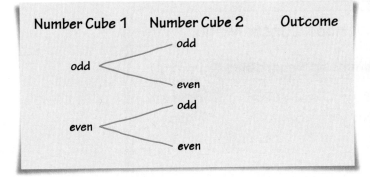

  a. List all the outcomes for the sums.

  b. Design rules for a two-player game that is fair.

  c. Design rules for a two-player game that is not fair.

  d. How is this situation similar to tossing two coins and seeing if the coins match or don't match?

11. Melissa is designing a birthday card for her sister. She has a blue, a yellow, a pink, and a green sheet of paper. She also has a black, a red, and a purple marker. Suppose Melissa chooses one sheet of paper and one marker at random.

  a. Make a tree diagram to find all the possible color combinations.

  b. What is the probability that Melissa chooses pink paper and a red marker?

  c. What is the probability that Melissa chooses blue paper? What is the probability she does not choose blue paper?

  d. What is the probability that she chooses a purple marker?

12. Lunch at school consists of a sandwich, a vegetable, and a fruit. Each lunch combination is equally likely to be given to a student. The students do not know what lunch they will get. Sol's favorite lunch is a chicken sandwich, carrots, and a banana.

> ### School Lunch Menu
>
> | Sandwiches | Vegetables | Fruit |
> | --- | --- | --- |
> | Chicken | Carrots | Apple |
> | Hamburger | Spinach | Banana |
> | Turkey | | |

a. Make a tree diagram to determine how many different lunches are possible. List all the possible outcomes.

b. What is the probability that Sol gets his favorite lunch? Explain your reasoning.

c. What is the probability that Sol gets at least one of his favorite lunch items? Explain.

13. Suppose you spin the pointer of the spinner at the right once and roll the number cube. (The numbers on the cube are 1, 2, 3, 4, 5, and 6.)

a. Make a tree diagram of the possible outcomes of a spin of the pointer and a roll of the number cube.

b. What is the probability that you get a 2 on both the spinner and the number cube? Explain your reasoning.

c. What is the probability that you get a *factor* of 2 on both the spinner and the number cube?

d. What is the probability that you get a *multiple* of 2 on both the number cube and the spinner?

Connections

14. Find numbers that make each sentence true.

a. $\frac{1}{8} = \frac{\blacksquare}{32} = \frac{5}{\blacksquare}$

b. $\frac{3}{7} = \frac{\blacksquare}{21} = \frac{6}{\blacksquare}$

c. $\frac{8}{20} = \frac{\blacksquare}{5} = \frac{16}{\blacksquare}$

15. Which of the following sums is equal to 1?

a. $\frac{1}{6} + \frac{3}{6} + \frac{2}{6}$

b. $\frac{4}{18} + \frac{1}{9} + \frac{2}{3}$

c. $\frac{1}{5} + \frac{1}{3} + \frac{1}{5}$

16. Describe a situation in which events have a theoretical probability that can be represented by the equation $\frac{1}{12} + \frac{1}{3} + \frac{7}{12} = 1$.

17. Kara and Bly both perform an experiment. Kara gets a probability of $\frac{125}{300}$ for a particular outcome. Bly gets a probability of $\frac{108}{320}$.

a. Whose experimental probability is closer to the theoretical probability of $\frac{1}{3}$? Explain your reasoning.

b. Give two possible experiments that Kara and Bly can do and that have a theoretical probability of $\frac{1}{3}$.

For Exercises 18–25, estimate the probability that the given event occurs. Any probability must be between 0 and 1 (or 0% and 100%). If an event is impossible, the probability it will occur is 0, or 0%. If an event is certain to happen, the probability it will occur is 1, or 100%.

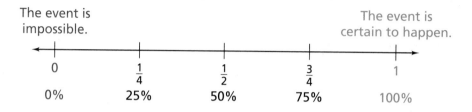

Sample

> Samantha: I watch some television every night, unless I have too much homework. So far, I do not have much homework today. I am about 95% sure that I will watch television tonight.

18. You are absent from school at least one day during this school year.

19. You have pizza for lunch one day this week.

20. It snows on July 4 this year in Mexico.

21. You get all the problems on your next math test correct.

22. The next baby born in your local hospital is a girl.

23. The sun sets tonight.

24. You take a turn in a game by tossing four coins. The result is all heads.

25. You toss a coin and get 100 tails in a row.

26. Karen and Mia play games with coins and number cubes. No matter which game they play, Karen loses more often than Mia. Karen is not sure if she just has bad luck or if the games are unfair. The games are described in this table. Review the game rules and complete the table.

Game	Can Karen Win?	Karen Likely to Win?	Game Fair or Unfair?
Game 1 Roll a number cube. • Karen scores a point if the roll is even. • Mia scores a point if the roll is odd.			
Game 2 Roll a number cube. • Karen scores a point if the roll is a multiple of 4. • Mia scores a point if the roll is a multiple of 3.			
Game 3 Toss two coins. • Karen scores a point if the coins match. • Mia scores a point if the coins do not match.			
Game 4 Roll two number cubes. • Karen scores a point if the number cubes match. • Mia scores a point if the number cubes do not match.			
Game 5 Roll two number cubes. • Karen scores a point if the product of the two numbers is 7. • Mia scores a point if the sum of the two numbers is 7.			

27. Karen and Mia invent another game. They roll a number cube twice and read the two digits shown as a two-digit number. So, if Karen gets a 6 and then a 2, she has 62.

Roll 1: 6

Roll 2: 2

Result: 62

a. What is the least number possible?

b. What is the greatest number possible?

c. Are all numbers equally likely?

d. Suppose Karen wins on any prime number and Mia wins on any multiple of 4. Explain how to decide who is more likely to win.

Multiple Choice For Exercises 28–31, choose the fraction closest to the given decimal.

28. 0.39

    A. $\frac{1}{2}$ **B.** $\frac{1}{4}$ **C.** $\frac{1}{8}$ **D.** $\frac{1}{10}$

29. 0.125

    F. $\frac{1}{2}$ **G.** $\frac{1}{4}$ **H.** $\frac{1}{8}$ **J.** $\frac{1}{10}$

30. 0.195

    A. $\frac{1}{2}$ **B.** $\frac{1}{4}$ **C.** $\frac{1}{8}$ **D.** $\frac{1}{10}$

31. 0.24

    F. $\frac{1}{2}$ **G.** $\frac{1}{4}$ **H.** $\frac{1}{8}$ **J.** $\frac{1}{10}$

32. Koto's class makes the line plot shown below. Each mark represents the first letter of the name of a student in her class.

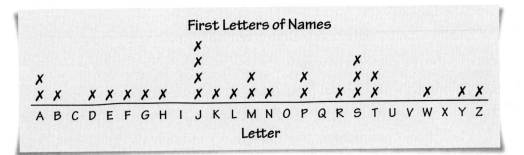

First Letters of Names

Suppose you choose a student at random from Koto's Class.

  a. What is the probability that the student's name begins with J?

  b. What is the probability that the student's name begins with a letter after F and before T in the alphabet?

  c. What is the probability that you choose Koto?

  d. Suppose two new students, Melvin and Theo, join the class. You now choose a student at random from the class. What is the probability that the student's name begins with J?

33. A bag contains red, white, blue, and green marbles. The probability of choosing a red marble is $\frac{1}{7}$. The probability of choosing a green marble is $\frac{1}{2}$. The probability of choosing a white marble is half the probability of choosing a red one. You want to find the number of marbles in the bag.

  a. Why do you need to know how to multiply and add fractions to proceed?

  b. Why do you need to know about multiples of whole numbers to proceed?

  c. Can there be seven marbles in the bag? Explain.

34. Write the following as one fraction.

  a. $\frac{1}{2}$ of $\frac{1}{7}$

  b. $\frac{1}{7} + \frac{1}{14} + \frac{1}{2}$

Extensions

35. Place 12 objects of the same size and shape, such as blocks or marbles, in a bag. Use three or four different solid colors.

    a. Describe the contents of your bag.

    b. Determine the theoretical probability of choosing each color by examining the bag's contents.

    c. Conduct an experiment to determine the experimental probability of choosing each color. Describe your experiment and record your results.

    d. How do the two types of probability compare?

36. Suppose you toss four coins.

    a. List all the possible outcomes.

    b. What is the probability of each outcome?

    c. Design a game for two players that involves tossing four coins. What is the probability that each player wins? Is one player more likely to win than the other player?

37. Suppose you are a contestant on the *Gee Whiz Everyone Wins!* game show in Problem 2.4. You win a mountain bike, a vacation to Hawaii, and a one-year membership to an amusement park. You play the bonus round and lose. Then the host makes this offer:

Would you accept this offer? Explain.

38. Suppose you compete for the bonus prize on the *Gee Whiz Everyone Wins!* game in Problem 2.4. You choose one block from each of two bags. Each bag contains one red, one yellow, and one blue block.

a. Make a tree diagram to show all the possible outcomes.

b. What is the probability that you choose two blocks that are *not* blue?

c. Jason made the tree diagram shown below to find the probability of choosing two blocks that are not blue. Using his tree, what probability do you think Jason got?

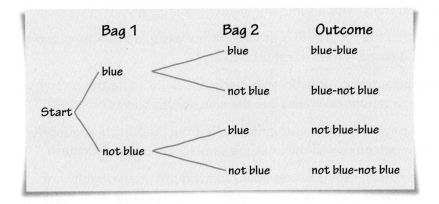

d. Does your answer in part (b) match Jason's? If not, why do you think Jason gets a different answer?

Mathematical Reflections 2

In this Investigation, you explored two ways to get information about probability. One method is to design an experiment and collect data. (The result is an experimental probability.) The other method is to analyze a situation carefully to see exactly what might happen. (The result is a theoretical probability.) The questions below will help you summarize what you have learned.

Think about these questions. Discuss your ideas with other students and your teacher. Then write a summary of your findings in your notebook.

1. **Describe** how you can find the theoretical probability of an outcome. **Why** is it called a theoretical probability?

2. **a.** Suppose two people do an experiment to estimate the probability of an outcome. Will they get the same probabilities? **Explain**.

   b. Two people analyze a situation to find the theoretical probability of an outcome. Will they get the same probabilities? **Explain**.

   c. One person uses an experiment to estimate the probability of an outcome. Another person analyzes the situation to find the theoretical probability of the outcome. Will they get the same probabilities? **Explain**.

3. **What** does it mean for a game to be fair?

4. **What** is a sample space, and how can it be represented?

Common Core Mathematical Practices

As you worked on the Problems in this Investigation, you used prior knowledge to make sense of them. You also applied Mathematical Practices to solve the Problems. Think back over your work, the ways you thought about the Problems, and how you used Mathematical Practices.

Shawna described her thoughts in the following way:

> In Problem 2.2, we had to decide if Jakayla or Adsila was correct about the probability of choosing a blue marble.
>
> Once we decided which girl was correct, we had to justify why we chose that student. We agreed with Adsila, since the probability is always less than or equal to 1. It cannot be greater than 1.
>
> ···
>
> **Common Core Standards for Mathematical Practice**
>
> **MP3** Construct viable arguments and critique the reasoning of others.

- What other Mathematical Practices can you identify in Shawna's reasoning?

- Describe a Mathematical Practice that you and your classmates used to solve a different Problem in this Investigation.

Making Decisions with Probability

Spring vacation has arrived! Kalvin thinks he can stay up until 11:00 P.M. every night. His father thinks Kalvin will have more energy for his activities during the vacation if he goes to bed at 9:00 P.M.

3.1 Designing a Spinner to Find Probabilities

Kalvin makes the three spinners shown below. Kalvin is negotiating with his father to use one of the spinners to determine his bedtime.

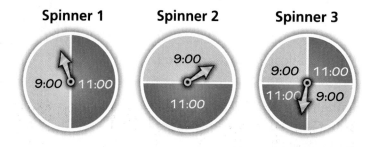

Spinner 1   Spinner 2   Spinner 3

- Which spinner gives Kalvin the best chance of going to bed at 11:00? Explain your reasoning.

Common Core State Standards

7.SP.C.7 Develop a probability model and use it to find probabilities of events. Compare probabilities from a model to observed frequencies . . .

7.SP.C.7b Develop a probability model (which may not be uniform) by observing frequencies in data generated from a chance process.

7.SP.C.8c Design and use a simulation to generate frequencies for compound events.

Also 7.RP.A.2, 7.RP.A.2a, 7.RP.A.3, 7.SP.C.5, 7.SP.C.6, 7.SP.C.7a, 7.SP.C.8, 7.SP.C.8a, 7.SP.C.8b

Problem 3.1

A Kalvin decides to design a spinner that lands on 11:00 most often. To convince his father to use this spinner, Kalvin puts three 9:00 spaces, two 10:00 spaces, and one 11:00 space on the spinner. However, he uses the biggest space for 11:00. Kalvin hopes the pointer lands on that space most often.

1. Which time do you think is most likely to occur?

2. Is Kalvin's father likely to agree to use this spinner? Explain why or why not.

B 1. Find the experimental probability that the pointer lands on 9:00, on 10:00, and on 11:00.

2. After how many spins did you decide to stop spinning? Explain why.

3. Suppose Kalvin spins the pointer 64 times. Based on your experiment, how many times can he expect the pointer to land on 9:00, on 10:00, and on 11:00?

C 1. What is the theoretical probability that the pointer lands on 9:00, on 10:00, and on 11:00? Explain.

2. Compare your answers to Question B, part (3) and Question C, part (1).

3. Suppose Kalvin spins the pointer 64 times. Based on your theoretical probabilities, how many times can he expect the pointer to land on 9:00, on 10:00, and on 11:00?

D Describe one way Kalvin's father can design a spinner so that Kalvin is most likely to go to bed at 9:00.

A C E Homework starts on page 58.

3.2 Making Decisions
Analyzing Fairness

One day at school, Kalvin's teacher has to decide which student to send to the office for an important message. Billie, Evo, and Carla volunteer. Kalvin suggests they design a quick experiment to choose the student fairly.

- What does it mean to choose the student fairly?

Problem 3.2

A 1. How could the class use each of these ways to choose a messenger?

    a. a coin   **b.** a number cube   **c.** colored cubes

    d. playing cards   **e.** a spinner   **f.** drawing straws

    2. Is each a fair way to make a choice? Explain why or why not.

In Questions B and C, three suggestions for making a decision are given. Decide whether each suggestion is a fair way to make the decision. If not, explain why.

B At lunch, Kalvin and his friends discuss whether to play kickball, soccer, baseball, or dodgeball. Ethan, Ava, and Beno all have suggestions.

Ethan: We can make a spinner like this.

Ava: We can roll a number cube. If it lands on 1, we play kickball. If it lands on 2, we play soccer. Landing on 3 means baseball, 4 means dodgeball, and we can roll again if it's a 5 or a 6.

Beno: We can put 1 red straw, 2 yellow straws, 3 green straws, and 4 purple straws in a container. If the straw drawn is red, we play soccer, and if it's yellow, we play baseball. If it's green, we play dodgeball, and if it's purple, we play kickball.

    1. Which method would you choose and why?

    2. Which method would you *not* choose and why?

    3. Are all three methods fair?

Problem **3.2** *continued*

C The group decides to play baseball. Tony and Meda are the team captains. Now they must decide who bats first. Examine each method, and then decide which method you would choose. Explain why.

Tony: We can roll a number cube. If the number is a multiple of 3, my team bats first. Otherwise, Meda's team bats first.

Meda: Yes, let's roll a number cube, but my team bats first if the number is even and Tony's team bats first if it's odd.

Jack: Each team rolls two number cubes, and the team that rolls two numbers that add to make an even number bats first.

D There are 60 sixth-grade students at Kalvin's school. The students need to choose someone to wear the mascot costume on field day. Huey and Sal are texting about it.

> We can give everyone a number from 1 to 60. Then, we can roll 10 number cubes and add the results. The person whose number is equal to the sum wears the costume. – Huey

> That doesn't seem fair. How about this?
>
> Everyone gets a number from 0 to 59. Put blocks numbered 0 to 5 in a bag. In another bag, put blocks numbered 0 to 9. Pick a block from the first bag for the tens digit and a block from the second bag for the ones digit. – Sal

1. Is Huey's plan unfair, as Sal claims? If so, why is it unfair?

2. Is Sal's plan fair or unfair? Explain your answer.

3. a. Design a new and fair plan for choosing someone to wear the mascot costume.

   b. Explain why your new plan will work.

A C E Homework starts on page 58.

3.3 Roller Derby
Analyzing a Game

 Have you ever figured out a strategy for winning a game?

Now that you know about making tables and diagrams to find probabilities, you can use these tools to find winning strategies for games. In this Problem, you play a two-team game called Roller Derby.

Each team needs a game board with columns numbered 1–12, a pair of number cubes, and 12 markers (such as coins, buttons, or small blocks).

- As you play, think about strategies for winning and how probability relates to your strategies.

Roller Derby

Rules

1. Each team places its 12 markers into their columns in any way it chooses.

2. Each team rolls a number cube. The team with the highest roll goes first.

3. Teams take turns rolling the two number cubes. They remove a marker from the column on their board with the same number as the sum of the numbers on the number cubes. If the column is empty, the team does not get to remove a marker.

4. The first team to remove all the markers from its board wins.

Problem 3.3

A
1. Play the game at least twice. For each game, record the strategies you use to place your markers on the board.

2. Record how many times each sum is rolled.

3. Which sums seem to occur most often?

4. Which sums do not come up very often?

5. What is a good strategy for placing your markers on the game board?

B
1. Find all the possible pairs of numbers you can get from rolling two number cubes.

2. Find the sum for each of these outcomes.

3. Are all of the sums equally likely? Explain.

4. How many ways can you get a sum of 2?

5. What is the probability of getting a sum of 4?

6. What is the probability of getting a sum of 6?

7. Which sums occur most often?

C Now that you have looked at the possible outcomes of the Roller Derby game, do you have any new strategies for winning? Explain.

 Homework starts on page 58.

Did You Know?

Galileo was an Italian physicist, astronomer, and mathematician. Among other things, he is famous for discovering the moons of Jupiter. He also studied problems in probability similar to the ones you have seen.

A famous problem he worked on involved rolling three number cubes. He looked at the possibilities for getting a sum of 9 or a sum of 10. A sum of 9 is made using six groups of numbers:

(1, 2, 6), (1, 3, 5), (1, 4, 4), (2, 2, 5), (2, 3, 4), and (3, 3, 3).

A sum of 10 is made using six other groups of numbers:

(1, 3, 6), (1, 4, 5), (2, 2, 6), (2, 3, 5), (2, 4, 4), and (3, 3, 4).

What puzzled people is that, when they did experiments, the sum of 10 occurred more often. By making a diagram similar to a counting tree, Galileo showed the theoretical probability matched the experimental results. There are actually 25 combinations that have a sum of 9, and 27 combinations that have a sum of 10.

3.4 Scratching Spots
Designing and Using a Simulation

People in different kinds of jobs find simulations useful to their business. A **simulation** is a model used to find experimental probabilities when it is not possible to work with a real situation. For example, when the first astronauts flew in space, they practiced in simulators to give them a sense of what it would be like in space.

In this Problem, you will play a simple game to help you think about simulation. After you play the game, you will be challenged to create a simulation for a situation that interests you.

• In what other situations would a simulation be helpful?

Problem 3.4

Tawanda's Toys is having a contest. Any customer who spends at least $10 receives a scratch-off prize card.

- Each card has five silver spots that reveal the names of video games when you scratch them.

- Exactly two spots match on each card.

- A customer may scratch off only two spots on a card.

- If the spots match, the customer wins that video game.

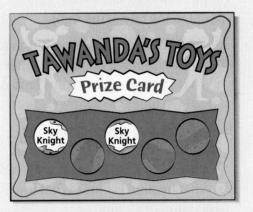

Prize cards are only given to paying customers. So, acquiring many of them for a valid experiment is not sensible. Instead, we can design an experiment using a model with the same characteristics as the prize cards. There are five equally likely choices, of which exactly two match. So, you can design an experiment using simulation to find the probability of each outcome.

One way you can simulate the scratch-off card is by using five playing cards, or by making your own cards. First, make sure that exactly two out of the five cards match. Place the cards facedown on a table. With your eyes closed, have a friend mix up the cards. Then open your eyes and choose two cards. If the cards match, you win. Otherwise, you lose.

A Use a simulation to find the experimental probability of winning.

B Examine the different ways you can scratch off two spots. Then use what you found to determine the theoretical probability of winning.

C **1.** How much do you need to spend to get 100 prize cards?

  2. How many video games can you expect to win with 100 prize cards?

D Describe a situation in which it would be very difficult to directly determine the probability of an event happening. Show how you could use simulation to help you figure out the approximate probabilities for the outcomes of the event.

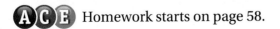 Homework starts on page 58.

Applications

1. For parts (a)–(g), use a spinner similar to the one at the right.

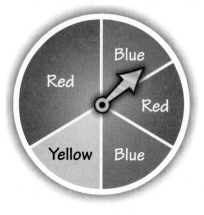

   a. Use a paper clip or bobby pin as a pointer. Spin the pointer 30 times. What fraction of your spins land on red? On blue? On yellow?

   b. Use an angle ruler or another method to examine the spinner. What fraction of the spinner is red? What fraction is blue? What fraction is yellow? Explain.

   c. Compare your answers to parts (a) and (b). Do you expect these answers to be the same? Explain why or why not.

   d. Suppose you spin 300 times instead of 30 times. Do you expect your answers to become closer to or further from the fractions you found in part (b)? Explain your reasoning.

   e. When you spin, is it equally likely that the pointer will land on red, on blue, or on yellow? Explain.

   f. Suppose you use the spinner to play a game with a friend. Your friend scores a point every time the pointer lands on red. To make the game fair, for what outcomes should you score a point? Explain.

   g. Suppose you use this spinner to play a three-person game. Player A scores if the pointer lands on yellow. Player B scores if the pointer lands on red. Player C scores if the pointer lands on blue. How can you assign points so the game is fair?

2. The cooks at Kyla's school make the spinners below to help them choose the lunch menu. They let the students take turns spinning. For parts (a)–(c), decide which spinner you would choose. Explain your reasoning.

Spinner A   **Spinner B**

a. Your favorite lunch is pizza.

b. Your favorite lunch is lasagna.

c. Your favorite lunch is hot dogs.

3. When you use each of the spinners below, the two possible outcomes are landing on 1 and landing on 2. Are the outcomes equally likely? If not, which outcome has a greater theoretical probability? Explain.

a.

b.

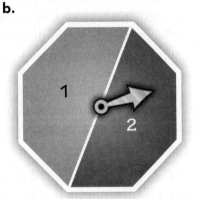

4. Molly designs a game for a class project. She makes the three spinners shown. She tests to see which one she likes best for her game. She spins each pointer 20 times and writes down her results, but she forgets to record which spinner gives which set of data. Match each spinner with one of the data sets. Explain your answer.

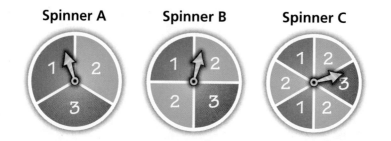

Spinner A   **Spinner B**   **Spinner C**

First data set: 1, 2, 3, 2, 1, 1, 2, 1, 2, 2, 2, 3, 2, 1, 2, 2, 2, 3, 2, 2

Second data set: 2, 3, 1, 1, 3, 3, 3, 1, 1, 2, 3, 2, 2, 2, 1, 1, 1, 3, 3, 3

Third data set: 1, 2, 3, 3, 1, 2, 2, 2, 3, 2, 1, 2, 2, 2, 3, 2, 2, 3, 2, 1

5. Three people play a game on each spinner in Exercise 4.
   Player 1 scores a point if the pointer lands on 1.
   Player 2 scores a point if the pointer lands on 2.
   Player 3 scores a point if the pointer lands on 3.

   a. On which spinner(s) is the game a fair game? Explain.

   b. Choose a spinner that you think doesn't make a fair game. Then, change the scoring rules to make the game fair by assigning different points for landing on the different numbers. Explain why your point system works.

6. **Multiple Choice** Jake, Carl, and John are deciding what to do after school. Jake thinks they should play video games. Carl wants to see a movie. John thinks they should ride their bikes. Which strategy is a fair way to decide?

   A. Let's toss three coins. If they all match, we play video games. If there are exactly two heads, we see a movie. If there are exactly two tails, we ride our bikes.

   B. Let's roll a number cube.
      If we roll a 1 or 2, we play video games.
      If we roll a 3 or 4, we go to the movies.
      Otherwise, we ride bikes.

   C. Let's use this spinner.

   D. None of these is fair.

7. **Multiple Choice** The Millers can't decide whether to eat pizza or burritos for dinner. Which strategy is a fair way to decide?

    F. Let's roll a number cube and toss a coin. If the number cube is even and the coin is heads, then we eat pizza. If the number cube is odd and the coin is tails, then we eat burritos. If neither happens, we try again.

    G. Let's toss a coin. If it is heads, we eat pizza. If it is tails, we do *not* eat burritos.

    H. Each of these is fair.

    J. Neither of these is fair.

8. **a.** Make a spinner and a set of rules for a fair two-person game. Explain why your game is fair.

    b. Make a spinner and a set of rules for a two-person game that is *not* fair. Explain why your game is not fair.

For Exercises 9 and 10, use your list of possible outcomes for rolling two number cubes from Problem 3.3.

9. **Multiple Choice** What is the probability of getting a sum of 5 when you roll two number cubes?

    A. $\frac{1}{9}$ **B.** $\frac{1}{6}$ **C.** $\frac{1}{4}$ **D.** $\frac{1}{3}$

10. **Multiple Choice** What is the probability of getting a sum greater than 9 when you roll two number cubes?

    F. $\frac{1}{9}$ **G.** $\frac{1}{6}$ **H.** $\frac{1}{4}$ **J.** $\frac{1}{3}$

Ella is playing Roller Derby with Carlos. Ella places all her markers in column 1 and Carlos places all of his markers in column 12.

11. **Multiple Choice** What is the probability that Ella will win?

    A. 0   **B.** $\frac{1}{3}$ **C.** $\frac{1}{2}$ **D.** 1

12. **Multiple Choice** What is the probability that Carlos will win?

    F. 0   **G.** $\frac{1}{3}$ **H.** $\frac{1}{2}$ **J.** 1

13. In some board games, you can end up in "jail." One way to get out of jail is to roll doubles (two number cubes that match). What is the probability of getting out of jail on your turn by rolling doubles? Use your list of possible outcomes of rolling two number cubes that you created for Problem 3.3. Explain your reasoning.

14. Tawanda wants fewer winners for her scratch-off cards. She decides to order new cards with six spots. Two of the spots on each card match. What is the probability that a person who plays once will win on the card?

Connections

Copy and complete the following table. Write each probability as a fraction, decimal, or percent.

Probabilities

	Fraction	Decimal	Percent
15.	$\frac{1}{4}$	▩	25%
16.	$\frac{1}{8}$	▩	▩
17.	▩	▩	$33\frac{1}{3}\%$
18.	▩	▩	10%
19.	▩	0.1666...	▩
20.	▩	0.05	▩

21. The cooks at Kyla's school let students make spinners to determine the lunch menu.

    a. Make a spinner for which the chance of selecting lasagna is 25%, the chance of selecting a hamburger is $16\frac{2}{3}$%, and the chance of selecting a tuna sandwich is $33\frac{1}{3}$%. The last choice is hot dogs.

    b. What is the chance of selecting hot dogs?

22. Three of the following situations have the same probability of getting "spinach." What is the probability for these three situations?

    a. Spin the pointer on this spinner once.

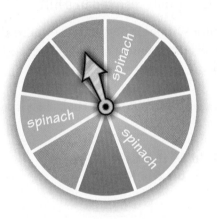

    b. Roll a number cube once. You get spinach when you roll a multiple of 3.

    c. Toss two coins. You get spinach with one head and one tail.

    d. Roll a number cube once. You get spinach when you roll a 5 or 6.

Rewrite each pair of numbers. Insert $<$, $>$, or $=$ to make a true statement.

    23. $\dfrac{1}{3\frac{1}{2}}$ ▇ $\dfrac{1}{4}$

    24. $\dfrac{3.5}{7}$ ▇ $\dfrac{1}{2}$

    25. 0.30 ▇ $\dfrac{1}{3}$

26. Use the table of historic baseball statistics to answer parts (a)–(d).

Batting Averages

Player	At-bats	Hits
Player A	4,089	1,317
Player B	5,457	1,715
Player C	4,877	1,518

a. What percent of Player A's at-bats resulted in a hit?

b. What percent of Player B's at-bats resulted in a hit?

c. What percent of Player C's at-bats resulted in a hit?

d. Suppose each player comes to bat today with the same skill his record shows. Who has the greatest chance of getting a hit? Explain your reasoning.

27. A–1 Trucks used this graph to show that their trucks last longer than other trucks.

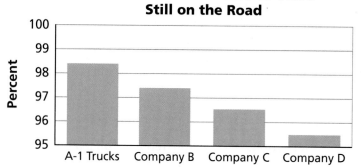

Trucks Sold in the Last 10 Years Still on the Road

a. The bar for A–1 Trucks is about six times the height of the bar for Company D. Does this mean that the chance of one of A–1's trucks lasting ten years is about six times as great as the chance of one of Company D's trucks lasting ten years? Explain.

b. If you wanted to buy a truck, would this graph convince you to buy a truck from A–1 Trucks? Why or why not?

For Exercises 28–30, find an equivalent fraction with a denominator of 10 or 100. Then, write a decimal number for each fraction.

28. $\frac{3}{20}$

29. $\frac{2}{5}$

30. $\frac{11}{25}$

31. Aran knows that if you roll a number cube once, there is a 50% chance of getting an even number. He says that if you roll a number cube twice, the chance of getting at least one even number is doubled. Is he correct?

32. **a.** Suppose you fold this shape along the dashed lines to make a three-dimensional shape. How many faces will it have?

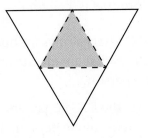

   b. Suppose you roll the shape in part (a). What is the probability that the shaded face lands on the bottom?

   c. Suppose you fold the below. Can you use it in a fair game in which you roll it? Explain.

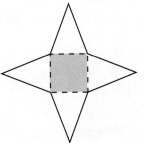

Use your list of possible outcomes when you roll two number cubes from Problem 3.3.

33. What is the probability that the sum is a multiple of 4?

34. What is the probability that the sum is a common multiple of 2 and 3?

35. What is the probability that the sum is a prime number? Explain.

36. Which has a greater probability of being rolled on a pair of number cubes, a sum that is a factor of 6 or a sum that is a multiple of 6? Explain your reasoining.

37. Suppose Humberto and Nina play the game Evens and Odds. They roll two number cubes and find the product of the numbers. If the product is odd, Nina scores a point. If the product is even, Humberto scores a point.

    a. Make a table of the possible products of two number cubes.

    b. What is the probability that Nina wins? What is the probability that Humberto wins? Explain your reasoning.

    c. Is this a fair game? If not, how could you change the points scored by each player so that it would be fair?

    d. What is the probability that the product is a prime number?

    e. What is the probability that the product is a factor of 4?

38. The Federal Trade Commission (FTC) makes rules for businesses that buy and sell things. One rule states that an advertisement may be found unlawful if it can deceive a person.

To decide whether an ad is deceptive, the FTC considers the "general impression" it makes on a "reasonable person." Even if every statement is true, the ad is deceptive if it gives an overall false impression. For example, cows can't appear in margarine ads because they give the false impression that margarine is a dairy product.

    a. Tawanda places this ad in a newspaper. According to the FTC, is it legal for Tawanda to say, "Every card is a winner"? Explain.

    b. Design a better ad that excites people but does not lead some to think they will win every time.

    c. Find an ad that might be deceptive. Why do you think it is deceptive? What proof could the company provide to change your mind?

39. A sugarless gum company used to have an advertisement that included the following statement:

> Four out of five dentists surveyed recommend sugarless gum for their patients who chew gum.

Do you think this statement means that 80% of dentists believe their patients should chew sugarless gum? Explain your reasoning.

40. Portland Middle School students make a flag as shown. After it hangs outside for a month, it looks dirty, and they examine it. They find more insects stuck on the yellow part than on the green part. Cheng says insects are more attracted to yellow than to green.

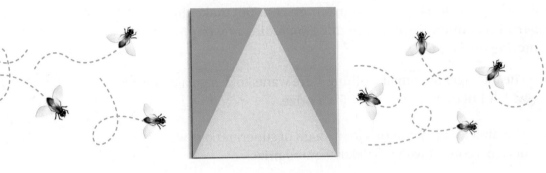

a. Students in a science class test Cheng's idea. They simulate the flag by using a piece of plywood painted with the same design. What is the chance that an insect landing at random on the plywood will hit the yellow part?

b. Suppose the result of the students' simulation is that 13 insects land on the yellow part and 12 insects land on the green part. Does this evidence support Cheng's conjecture?

Extensions

41. Design a spinner with five regions. You want the pointer to be equally likely to land in all of the regions. Give the number of degrees in the central angle of each region.

42. Design a spinner with five regions such that the chance of landing in one region is twice the chance of landing in each of the other four regions. Give the number of degrees in the central angle of each region.

For Exercises 43–45, design a contest for each company. Each contest should help the company attract customers, but not make the company lose money. Explain the rules, including any requirements for entering the contest.

43. The manager of a small clothing store wants to design a contest in which 1 of every 30 players wins a prize.

44. The director of operations for a chain of supermarkets wants to design a contest with a $100,000 grand prize!

45. An auto dealer sells new and used cars. The owner wants to have a contest with many winners and big prizes. She wants about one of every ten players to win a $500 prize.

Mathematical Reflections 3

In this Investigation, you used spinners and number cubes in probability situations. You used both experimental and theoretical probabilities to help you make decisions. You also examined a game to determine winning strategies for playing the game. The questions below will help you summarize what you learned.

Think about these questions. Discuss your ideas with other students and your teacher. Then write a summary of your findings in your notebook.

1. **Describe** a situation in which you and a friend can use probability to make a decision. Can the probabilities of the outcomes be determined both experimentally and theoretically? **Why** or why not?

2. **Describe** a situation in which it is difficult or impossible to find the theoretical probabilities of the outcomes.

3. **Explain** what it means for a probability situation to be fair.

4. **Describe** some of the strategies for determining the theoretical probabilities for situations in this Unit. Give an example of a situation for each of the strategies.

Common Core Mathematical Practices

As you worked on the Problems in this Investigation, you used prior knowledge to make sense of them. You also applied Mathematical Practices to solve the Problems. Think back over your work, the ways you thought about the Problems, and how you used Mathematical Practices.

Ken described his thoughts in the following way:

We were making decisions about fairness in Problem 3.2. We had several tools:

- coin
- colored cubes
- spinner
- number cube
- playing cards
- drawing straws

We had to determine which one was the most reasonable for choosing a messenger.

We also explained how we decided each tool was fair or not. To determine the fairness of each tool, we had to understand how each tool was used. We wanted to make sure each of the three students had the same chance of being chosen.

Our group used a number cube. Billie goes if 1 or 2 comes up. Evo goes if 3 or 4 comes up. Carla goes if 5 or 6 comes up. As a class, we found a way to make each tool work.

Common Core Standards for Mathematical Practice

MP5 Use appropriate tools strategically.

? • What other Mathematical Practices can you identify in Ken's reasoning?

• Describe a Mathematical Practice that you and your classmates used to solve a different Problem in this Investigation.

Analyzing Compound Events Using an Area Model

Each turn in the games of chance in Investigation 3 involved two actions. Recall the Roller Derby game in Problem 3.3. In this game, you rolled two number cubes and then determined the outcomes. You determined the theoretical probabilities of these games using a variety of strategies.

Situations involving chance occur in many of the games we love to play. We always want to know what our chances are of winning in each situation. It helps if we have some ideas that help us analyze a situation.

An area model is a useful tool for analyzing situations with two stages. The goal is to divide the area into parts that correctly reflect the chances we have to win.

In this Investigation, you encounter probability situations that involve more than one action on a turn.

Common Core State Standards

7.SP.C.6. Approximate the probability of a chance event by collecting data on the chance process that produces it and observing its long-run relative frequency, and predict the approximate relative frequency given the probability.

7.SP.C.7b. Develop a probability model (which may not be uniform) by observing frequencies in data generated from a chance process.

7.SP.C.8. Find probabilities of compound events using organized lists, tables, tree diagrams, and simulation.

7.SP.C.8c Design and use a simulation to generate frequencies for compound events.

Also 7.RP.A.2, 7.RP.A.2a, 7.RP.A.3, 7.SP.C.5, 7.SP.C.7, 7.SP.C.7a, 7.SP.C.8a, 7.SP.C.8b

4.1 Drawing Area Models to Find the Sample Space

Bucket 1 contains three marbles—one red and two green. Bucket 2 contains four marbles—one red, one blue, one green, and one yellow. The player draws a marble from each bucket.

Bucket 1

Bucket 2

> ? How can we analyze this two-stage situation so that we can predict what outcomes can occur and with what frequency?

Problem 4.1

Miguel draws a square to represent an area of 1 square unit. He will use the square's area to represent a probability of 1. The square represents the sum of all of the probabilities for all of the possible outcomes.

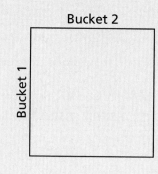

Bucket 2

Bucket 1

What Do You Expect?

Problem 4.1 continued

A Miguel adds to his diagram to help him find the theoretical probabilities of drawing marbles from Bucket 1.

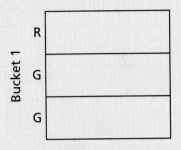

1. Explain what Miguel has done so far. Does this look reasonable?

2. Use the top edge to represent Bucket 2. How many sections do you need to represent the marbles in Bucket 2? Draw the lines and label the sections you need to represent Bucket 2.

3. Now label each of the sections inside the square with two letters to represent the results of choosing two marbles. RR in a section would mean that two red marbles were drawn from the buckets.

B Use your probability area model from Question A to answer each part.

1. What are the probabilities for selecting each pair of marbles?

   a. RR   **b.** RB   **c.** RG

   d. RY   **e.** GR   **f.** GB

   g. GG   **h.** GY   **i.** YY

2. Use your drawing to answer these questions:

   What is the probability of choosing a marble from each bucket and

   a. getting at least one red?

   b. getting at least one blue?

   c. getting at least one green?

   d. getting at least one yellow?

Problem 4.1 continued

C The area model below represents a different situation from Questions A and B. In this area model, $P(RY) = \frac{1}{10}$, $P(RB) = \frac{1}{10}$, $P(GY) = \frac{4}{10}$, and $P(GB) = \frac{4}{10}$. Use the area model and these probabilities to answer the following questions:

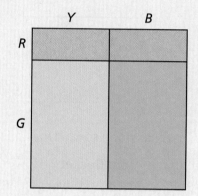

1. What is the area of each section?

2. For each section, what fraction of the whole square is this?

3. How do the fractions in part (2) compare to the probabilities of each section?

4. Which of the following could be the contents of the two buckets? Explain your reasoning.

    a. 2 red and 8 green in Bucket 1
        5 yellow and 5 blue in Bucket 2

    b. 2 red and 8 green in Bucket 1
        10 yellow and 10 blue in Bucket 2

    c. 1 red and 4 green in Bucket 1
        3 yellow and 3 blue in Bucket 2

A C E Homework starts on page 80.

4.2 Making Purple
Area Models and Probability

Making Purple is a popular game at the school carnival. A player spins the pointer of each spinner below once. Getting red on one spinner and blue on the other spinner wins, because red and blue together make purple.

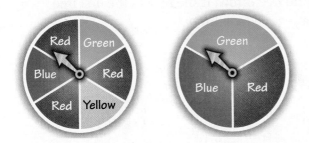

- Suppose you take ten turns with the two spinners. How often would you expect to get red and blue?

Problem 4.2

A Play the Making Purple game several times. Based on your results, what is the experimental probability that a player will "make purple" on a turn?

B Construct an area model. Determine the theoretical probability that a player will make purple on a turn.

C How do your answers to Questions A and B compare?

D The cost to play the game is $2. The winner gets $6 for making purple. Suppose 36 people play the game.

   1. How much money will the school take in from this game?

   2. How many people do you expect will win a prize?

   3. How much money do you expect the school to pay out in prizes?

   4. How much profit do you expect the school to make from this game?

   5. Should the school include this game in the carnival? Justify your answer using your answers to parts (1)–(4).

ACE Homework starts on page 80.

4.3 One-and-One Free Throws
Simulating a Probability Situation

In the district finals, Nishi's basketball team is 1 point behind with 2 seconds left. A player on the other team fouls Nishi. Now she is in a one-and-one free-throw situation. This means that Nishi will try one free throw. If she makes it, she tries a second free throw. If she misses the first free throw, she does not get to try a second free throw.

- What are the possible scores Nishi can make in a one-and-one free-throw situation?

- How can each score be made?

- How would you design an experiment to analyze this situation?

Problem 4.3

A
1. Is it most likely that Nishi will score 0 points, 1 point, or 2 points? Record what you think before you analyze the situation.

2. Is the spinner below a good model for Nishi's free-throw record? Explain your reasoning.

3. Simulate Nishi's one-and-one situation 20 times using a spinner like the one above. Record the result of each trial.

4. Based on your results, what is the experimental probability that Nishi will score 0 points? 1 point? 2 points?

B
1. Make an area model for this situation using a 10 × 10 grid. What is the theoretical probability that Nishi will score 0 points? 1 point? 2 points? Compare the three theoretical probabilities with the three experimental probabilities.

2. How does the spinner in Question A, part (2) reflect Nishi's free-throw record? How does the area model in Question B, part (1) reflect Nishi's free-throw record? Which of these models is the better model for Nishi's free-throw record? Explain.

3. Refer to the area model in Question B, part (1). How does this help you predict the number of times Nishi will score 2 points in 100 one-and-one situations? In 200 one-and-one situations?

C Suppose Nishi's free-throw percentage is 70%. Explain how the new percentage affects the outcome.

A **C** **E** Homework starts on page 80.

4.4 Finding Expected Value

In the last Problem, you looked at different probabilities. These probabilities represented different outcomes of Nishi's one-and-one free-throw situation. You might have been surprised about which outcome is most likely. In this Problem, you will look at the number of points Nishi can expect to make each time she is in a one-and-one free-throw situation.

- What is Nishi most likely to score? What is Nishi least likely to score?

The mean, or average, number of points for each one-and-one free-throw situation is called the **expected value.**

- What do you think her average score, or expected value, will be for a one-and-one free-throw situation?

Problem 4.4

Suppose Nishi has a 60% free-throw percentage and is in a one-and-one free-throw situation 100 times during the season.

(A) **1.** How many times can she expect to score 0 points? What is the total number of points for these situations?

2. How many times can she expect to score 1 point? What is the total number of points for these situations?

3. How many times can she expect to score 2 points? What is the total number of points for these situations?

4. What total number of points do you expect Nishi to score in these 100 situations at the free-throw line?

5. Find Nishi's average number of points for a one-and-one situation.

6. Use the data you collected from the spinner simulation in Problem 4.3. Calculate the average score for the experimental results for Nishi. How does the theoretical average compare with the experimental average?

Problem 4.4 *continued*

B **1.** Copy and complete the table below for the players whose free-throw percentages are 20%, 40%, 60%, and 80% in 100 one-and-one situations. You will fill in the Expected Value column in part (2).

**Points Expected in 100
One-and-One Situations**

Player's Free-Throw Percentage	Points			
	0	1	2	Expected Value, or Average
20%	■	■	■	■
40%	■	■	■	■
60%	■	■	■	■
80%	■	■	■	■

2. Calculate the mean, or average, number of points for each situation. Record these values in the table in part (1). Describe any patterns.

C **1.** Use the data from the table in Question B, part (1). Complete a graph like the one below.

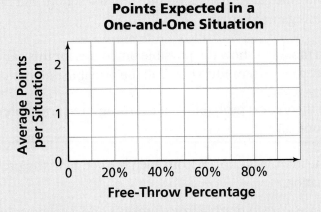

**Points Expected in a
One-and-One Situation**

2. How does the mean, or average, number of points compare for players with a 20% free-throw percentage? 40%? 60%? 80%?

3. Nishi's dad makes an average of about 1 point in each one-and-one free-throw situation. Find his free-throw percentage.

4. Nishi's older sister has a 70% free-throw percentage. What is her average number of points in a one-and-one situation? Check by making an area model.

ACE Homework starts on page 80.

Applications

A school carnival committee features a different version of the Making Purple game, as shown below.

Making Purple
$1 to play
Draw a red marble
and a blue marble.
Win $3!

marbles
● 1 red
○ 1 blue
○ 1 green
○ 1 yellow

marbles
● 1 red
○ 1 yellow
○ 1 green

1. Before playing the game, do you predict that the school will make money on this game? Explain.

2. Use an area model to show the possible outcomes for this game. Explain how your area model shows all the possible outcomes.

3. What is the theoretical probability of choosing a red and a blue marble on one turn?

4. Suppose one marble is chosen from each bucket. Find the probability of each situation.

   a. You choose a green marble from Bucket 1 and a yellow marble from Bucket 2.

   b. You do not choose a blue marble from either bucket.

   c. You choose two blue marbles.

   d. You choose at least one blue marble.

5. Parker Middle School is having a Flag Day Festival. In a contest, students choose one block from each of two different bags. A student wins if he or she picks a red and a blue block. James makes the tree diagram below to find the probability of winning.

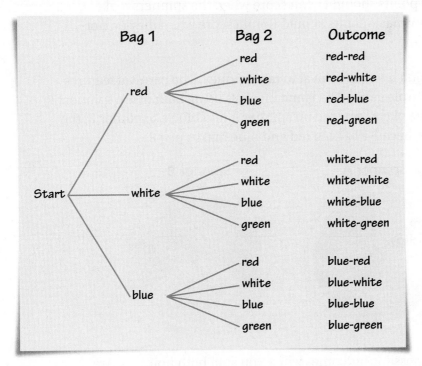

a. Draw an area model that represents this contest.

b. What is the probability of winning this contest?

6. There are two No-Cavity prize bins at a dentist's office. One bin has two hot-pink toothbrushes and three neon-yellow toothbrushes. The other bin has four packages of sugar-free gum, three grape and one strawberry. Kira has no cavities. The dentist tells her to close her eyes and choose a prize from each bin.

a. What is the probability that Kira will choose a neon-yellow toothbrush and a pack of grape gum? Draw an area model to support your solution.

b. The dental assistant refills the bins after every patient. Suppose the next 100 patients have no cavities. How many times do you expect the patients to get a neon-yellow toothbrush and a pack of grape gum?

7. Bonita and Deion are using the spinners from the Making Purple game in Problem 4.2. They take turns spinning. If the colors on the two spinners make purple, Deion scores. If the colors do not make purple, Bonita scores. They want to make their game a fair game. How many points should Deion score when the spinners make purple? How many points should Bonita score when they do not make purple?

8. A science club hosts a carnival to raise money. The carnival features a Making Purple game. The game involves using both of the spinners shown. If the player gets red on spinner A and blue on spinner B, the player wins, because mixing red and blue makes purple.

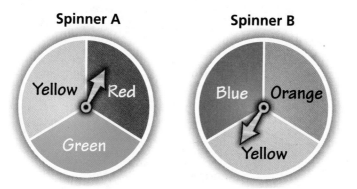

Spinner A

Yellow / Red
Green

Spinner B

Blue | Orange
Yellow

a. List the possible outcomes when you spin both pointers. Are these outcomes equally likely? Explain your reasoning.

b. What is the theoretical probability that a player "makes purple"? Show or explain how you arrived at your answer.

c. Suppose 100 people play the Making Purple game. How many people do you expect to win?

d. The club charges $1 per turn. A player who makes purple receives $5. The club expects 100 people to play. How much money do you expect the club to make?

For Exercises 9–11, a bag contains three green marbles and two blue marbles. You choose a marble, return it to the bag, and then choose again.

9. a. Which method (*make a tree diagram, make a list, use an area model,* or *make a table or chart*) would you use to find the possible outcomes? Explain your choice.

   b. Use your chosen method to find all of the possible outcomes.

10. Suppose you do this experiment 50 times. Predict the number of times you will choose two marbles of the same color. Use the method you chose in Exercise 9.

11. Suppose this experiment is a two-person game. One player scores if the marbles match. The other player scores if the marbles do not match. Describe a scoring system that makes this a fair game.

12. Al is at the top of Morey Mountain. He wants to make choices that will lead him to the lodge. He does not remember which trails to take.

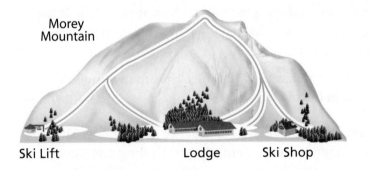

a. Design an experiment using a number cube or drawing the numbers 1–6 from a hat. Find the experimental probability of Al ending at the lodge. Conduct the experiment 20 times.

b. What is the experimental probability of Al ending at the lodge? At the lift? At the ski shop?

c. Find the theoretical probability of ending at the lodge, the lift, and the ski shop. Compare the experimental and theoretical probabilities. Do you have more confidence in the experimental or the theoretical probability? Why?

13. Kenisha is designing a game involving paths through the woods that lead to caves. A player first chooses Cave A or Cave B. Next, the player starts at the beginning and chooses a path at random at each fork. If the player lands in the cave that was chosen in the beginning, he or she wins a prize.

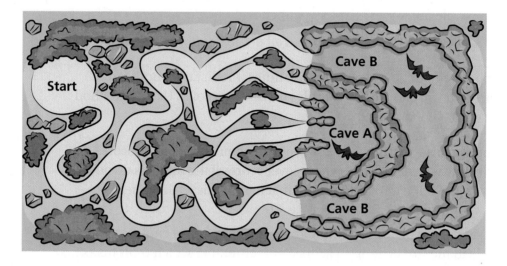

a. Suppose a player chooses a path at random at each fork. What is the theoretical probability that the player ends up in Cave A? In Cave B? Show or explain how you arrived at your answer.

b. Suppose you play this game 100 times. How many times do you expect to end in Cave A? In Cave B?

14. Kenisha designed another version of the cave paths game. The new version has a different arrangement of paths leading into Caves A and B. She makes an area model to analyze the probabilities of landing in each room. For Kenisha's new version, what is the probability that a player will end up in Cave A? In Cave B?

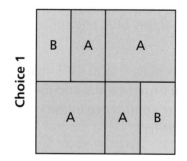

15. **Multiple Choice** Choose the map that the area model in Exercise 14 could represent.

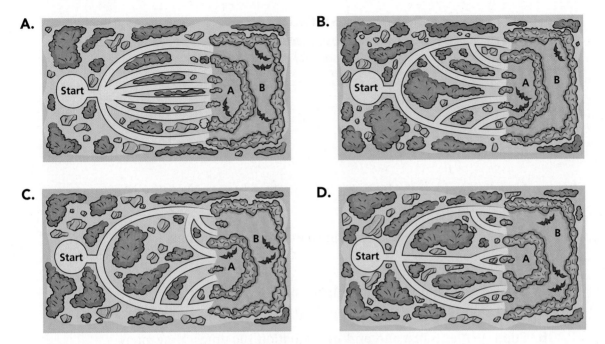

A.

B.

C.

D.

For Exercises 16 and 17, a basketball player participates in a one-and-one free-throw situation. Determine if each player with the given free-throw percentage will most likely score 0 points, 1 point, or 2 points. Make an area model to support each answer.

16. 80%

17. 40%

18. Nishi, who has a 60% free-throw percentage, is in a two-attempt free-throw situation. This means that she will attempt the second free throw no matter what happens on the first.

   a. Is Nishi most likely to score 0 points, 1 point, or 2 points? Explain.

   b. Nishi plans to keep track of her score on two-attempt free-throw situations. What average number of points can she expect to score per two-attempt situation?

19. Repeat Exercise 18 for a player with each free-throw percentage.

   a. 50%

   b. 80%

Use the information in the table. It shows free-throw statistics for some of the players on a basketball team.

Free-Throw Statistics

Name	Free Throws Attempted	Free Throws Made
Gerrit	54	27
David	49	39
Ken	73	45
Alex	60	42

20. **a.** Which player has the best chance of making his next free throw? Explain your reasoning.

  b. What is the probability of making a free throw on the next try for each person?

21. **a.** Alex is in a one-and-one free-throw situation. What is the probability he will score 0 points? 1 point? 2 points?

  b. Suppose Alex is in a one-and-one situation 100 times. How many times do you expect each outcome in part (a) to occur?

  c. What is the average number of points you expect Alex to make in a one-and-one situation?

  d. Repeat part (a) using Gerrit.

22. **a.** In a two-attempt free-throw situation, a player gets a second attempt even if the first attempt is missed. Suppose Gerrit is in a two-attempt free-throw situation. What is the probability that he will score 0 points? 1 point? 2 points?

  b. Compare your answers to Exercise 21. Explain why the answers are not exactly the same.

Connections

For Exercises 23–28, Megan is designing a computer game called *Treasure Hunt.* The computer chooses a square at random on the grid. Then, it hides a treasure in the room containing the square. Find the probability that the computer will hide the treasure in each room.

23. Library

24. Den

25. Dining hall

26. Great hall

27. Front hall

28. **Multiple Choice** Megan enlarges the floor plan in the game grid above by a scale factor of 2. How does this affect the probabilities that the treasure is in each room?

   F. They are unchanged.

   G. They are $\frac{1}{2}$ the original probability.

   H. They are twice the original.

   J. They are four times the original.

29. Carlos is also designing a *Treasure Hunt* game. He keeps track of the number of times the computer hides the treasure in each room. Here is a line plot of his results.

Dining Room	✗ ✗ ✗ ✗ ✗ ✗ ✗ ✗ ✗
Living Room	✗ ✗ ✗ ✗ ✗ ✗ ✗ ✗ ✗ ✗ ✗ ✗ ✗ ✗ ✗ ✗ ✗ ✗ ✗
Library	✗ ✗ ✗ ✗ ✗ ✗ ✗ ✗ ✗ ✗
Kitchen	✗ ✗ ✗ ✗
Front Hall	✗ ✗ ✗ ✗

Design a floor plan that could give this data. State the area of each room on your floor plan.

30. Seniors at a high school took a survey. The results are shown below.

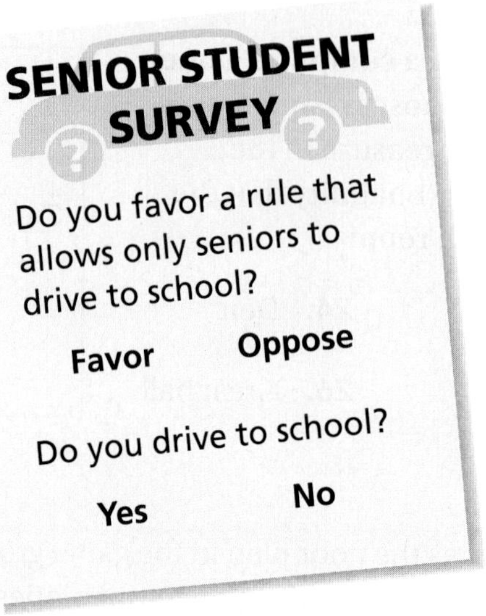

SENIOR STUDENT SURVEY

Do you favor a rule that allows only seniors to drive to school?

Favor Oppose

Do you drive to school?

Yes No

Driving Survey

	Drives to School	Does Not Drive to School	Row Totals
Favors Rule	40	30	70
Opposes Rule	20	10	30
Total	60	40	100

a. How many seniors drive to school?

b. How many seniors favor the rule?

c. How many seniors favor the rule and do not drive to school?

d. What is the probability that a senior chosen at random favors the rule?

e. What is the probability that a senior chosen at random drives to school and favors the rule?

f. What is the probability that a senior chosen at random drives to school or opposes the rule?

g. Are the results of this survey a good indicator of how all of the students at the high school feel about the driving rule? Explain.

31. Marni and Ira are playing a game with this square spinner. A game is ten turns. Each turn is two spins. The numbers for the two spins are added. Marni scores 1 point for a sum that is negative. Ira scores 1 point for a sum that is positive. After ten turns, each player totals their points. The player with more points wins.

    a. List all of the possible outcomes.

    b. Is this game fair? Explain.

32. Fergus designs a dartboard for a school carnival. His design is shown below. He must decide how much to charge a player and how much to pay out for a win. To do this, he needs to know the probabilities of landing in sections marked A and B. Assume the darts land at random on the dartboard.

A	A	A	A	A	A
A					A
A					A
A		B			A
A					A
A	A	A	A	A	A

    a. What is the probability of landing in a section marked A?

    b. What is the probability of landing in a section marked B?

33. Fergus designs two more dartboards for the school carnival. A player pays $1 to play and wins $2 if the dart lands in sections marked B. If the dart lands in sections marked A, the player wins no money.

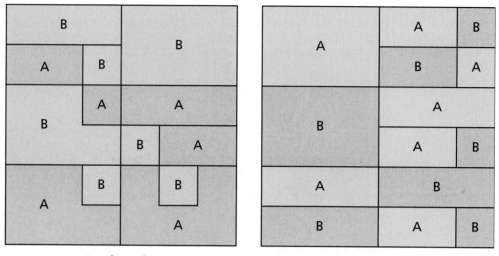

Dartboard 1   **Dartboard 2**

 a. What is the probability of landing in sections marked A on Dartboard 1? On Dartboard 2? Explain.

 b. How much money will the player expect to make (or lose) after 36 turns using Dartboard 1? Using Dartboard 2? Explain.

 c. How much money will the carnival expect to make (or lose) after 36 turns using Dartboard 1? Using Dartboard 2?

 d. Can the carnival expect to make a profit on this game with either board? Explain.

34. a. If you roll one number cube two times, what is the probability of getting a factor of 5 both times?

 b. Suppose you roll two different number cubes. What is the probability of getting a factor of 5 on both cubes?

 c. How do your answers to parts (a) and (b) compare? Explain why the answers have this relationship.

For Exercises 35–37, a game show uses a large spinner with many equal-sized sections. One section is labeled *Bankrupt*. If a player spins and lands on *Bankrupt*, she loses all of her money. Carlota makes a version of the spinner below. Answer each question and explain your reasoning.

35. What is the probability that a player who spins the spinner one time will land on *Bankrupt*?

36. What is the probability that a player who spins the spinner one time will get $500 or more?

37. Sam just spun the spinner and landed on $350. What is the probability he will land on $350 on his next spin?

Multiple Choice For Exercises 38–40, choose the answer that is the correct percent of the given number.

38. 30% of 90

    A. 60   **B.** 27   **C.** 30   **D.** 18

39. 25% of 80

    F. 20   **G.** 3.2   **H.** 15   **J.** 25

40. 45% of 180

    A. 70   **B.** 40   **C.** 81   **D.** 53

41. Wanda, the Channel 1 weather person, uses previous data and a computer model to predict the weather. By looking at many previous days with the same weather conditions, she saw that it rained 30 out of 100 days. So, she predicted that there is a 30% chance of rain on Saturday and a 30% chance of rain on Sunday. Then, it rained both days.

    a. Suppose Wanda's calculations were correct, and there was a 30% chance of rain each day. What was the probability that there would be rain on both days?

    b. How should Wanda explain this to her manager?

    c. Wanda is working on her predictions for the next few days. She calculates that there is a 20% chance of rain on Monday and a 20% chance of rain on Tuesday. If she is correct, what is the probability that it will rain on at least one of these days?

42. A lake has 10,000 fish. When a fisherman scoops up his net, he catches 500 fish. Suppose 150 of the 500 fish in his net are salmon. How many salmon do you predict are in the lake?

43. a. Copy the table below. Use your answers from Problem 4.5 to fill in your table.

Average Points per Attempt for Different Free-Throw Percentages

Probability of One Basket	20%	40%	60%	80%	100%
Average Points per One-and-One Attempt	0.24	▨	0.96	▨	▨

b. Is the average for an 80% percentage twice that of 40%? Explain.

c. Use this table or your graph from Problem 4.4, Question C. Is the average for 100% twice the average of 50%? Explain.

d. A player with a 20% free-throw percentage makes 0.24 points, on average, in a one-and-one situation. Copy and complete this table. How are the relationships in this table different from the table in part (a)?

Average Points for a Player With a 20% Free-Throw Percentage

Number of One-and-One Situations	1	10	20	100
Average Points Made	0.24	▨	▨	▨

Suppose you spin the pointer on each spinner once.

44. Suppose you add the results.

    a. What is the probability of getting a positive number?

    b. What is the average value?

45. Suppose you multiply the results.

    a. What is the probability of getting a positive number?

    b. What is the average value?

Extensions

Use the information below to answer Exercises 46–48.

Gee Whiz Everybody Wins!

Rules

One player waits backstage.

The other player places two green marbles and two blue marbles in two containers in any arrangement.

The player backstage comes out and chooses one of the containers at random.

The player chooses a marble at random without looking.

If the marble is green both players win a prize.

46. Suppose Brianna is given two green marbles and two blue marbles to distribute between the two containers. Emmanuel waits backstage.

   a. List all of the different ways Brianna can place the four marbles in the two containers.

   b. For each arrangement, what is the probability that Emmanuel chooses a green marble?

   c. Which arrangement will give Brianna and Emmanuel the greatest chance of winning? The least chance of winning? Explain.

47. Brianna is given two blue marbles and three green marbles to distribute between the two containers. Which arrangement gives Emmanuel the best chance of choosing a green marble?

48. Suppose Brianna is given two green marbles, two blue marbles, and three buckets. How can she put the marbles in the three buckets to have the best chance of choosing a green marble?

49. Della is chosen as a contestant on a game show. The host gives her two red marbles, two green marbles, and two yellow marbles.

Della will put the marbles into two identical cans in any way she chooses. The host will then rearrange the cans. He will leave the marbles as Della placed them. Della will then select a can and choose a marble. If she chooses a red marble, she wins a prize.

How should Della arrange the marbles so she has the best chance of choosing a red marble?

50. Make up your own marbles-and-buckets problem. Find the solution.

51. For the game below, you use the two spinners shown. You get two spins. You may spin each spinner once, or you may spin one of the spinners twice. If you get a red on one spin and a blue on the other spin (the order makes no difference), you win. To have the greatest chance of winning, should you spin Spinner A twice, spin Spinner B twice, or spin each spinner once? Explain.

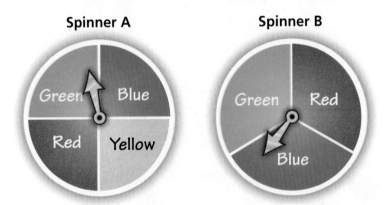

Spinner A: Green, Blue, Red, Yellow

Spinner B: Green, Red, Blue

Use the data about the basketball team from Exercises 20–22.

52. What is the probability that Alex will make all of his next three free throws? Explain your reasoning.

53. David is in a one-and-one free-throw situation. What is the probability that he will make both free throws?

54. Emilio increases his free-throw average to 50%. His coach makes a deal with him. At tomorrow's practice, Emilio can attempt either to make three free throws in a row or to make at least four out of five free throws. If he is successful, he will start every game for the rest of the season. Which option should he choose? Explain.

55. a. Curt has made 60% of his free throws during recent practice sessions. The coach says that if Curt makes three free throws in a row, he can start Saturday's game. What is the probability that Curt will start Saturday's game?

   b. Curt has a difficult time making three free throws in a row. The coach tells him to instead try making three out of four free throws. What is the probability that Curt will make at least three out of four free throws?

56. When a player is fouled while attempting a three-point basket, three free throws are awarded. Luis has an 80% free-throw percentage. He draws the diagrams below to analyze the probability of getting 1, 2, or 3 baskets.

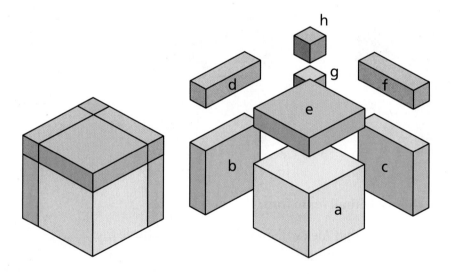

   a. Which parts of the lettered diagram represent Luis making all three baskets? Exactly two baskets? Exactly one basket? Missing all three baskets?

   b. What is the probability of Luis getting 1 point in a three free-throw situation? 2 points? 3 points? No points?

Mathematical Reflections 4

In this Investigation, you analyzed probabilities of two-stage events by dividing the area of a square. You also learned how to find the average outcome for events, such as a basketball player attempting free throws in a one-and-one situation. The following questions will help you summarize what you have learned.

Think about these questions. Discuss your ideas with other students and your teacher. Then write a summary of your findings in your notebook.

1. **Describe** four probability situations that involve two actions. **Describe** the outcomes for these situations.

2. You can use an area model or a simulation to determine the probability of a situation that involves two actions. **Explain** how each of these is used.

3. **Describe** how you would calculate the expected value for a probability situation.

4. Expected value is sometimes called the long-term average. **Explain** why this makes sense.

Common Core Mathematical Practices

As you worked on the Problems in this Investigation, you used prior knowledge to make sense of them. You also applied Mathematical Practices to solve the Problems. Think back over your work, the ways you thought about the Problems, and how you used Mathematical Practices.

Hector described his thoughts in the following way:

> We found the expected value for players with different free-throw percentages in Problem 4.4. We had to focus on the important information necessary to complete our table. Then we described the pattern we noticed in the data.
>
> For the players with 20%, 40%, 60%, and 80% free-throw percentages, we noticed that the numbers of missed baskets out of 100 were in reverse order (80, 60, 40, and 20).
>
> We thought about how the expected value increased by 0.48 when the free-throw percentage increased from 60% to 80%. We guessed that half of that increase would be from 60% to 70%. This gave us an estimated value of 1.2 for the expected value of a player with a 70% free-throw percentage.

Common Core Standards for Mathematical Practice

MP2 Reason abstractly and quantitatively.

? • What other Mathematical Practices can you identify in Hector's reasoning?

• Describe a Mathematical Practice that you and your classmates used to solve a different Problem in this Investigation.

Binomial Outcomes

In some situations, there are only two outcomes. In Investigation 1, you flipped a paper cup to determine which cereal Kalvin would eat for breakfast. The two outcomes, *end* or *side,* were not equally likely.

You also flipped a coin to determine which cereal Kalvin would eat for breakfast. The two outcomes, *heads* or *tails,* were equally likely.

- What are other examples of situations with two outcomes?

- Which of these are equally likely?

Situations like tossing a coin or a cup that have exactly two outcomes are binomial situations. If a situation has *n* identical trials and each trial results in one of two outcomes, then the probability of a given outcome is called a **binomial probability.**

- What are some other examples of binomial probability situations?

- What probability questions might you ask about these situations?

In this Investigation you will explore situations that are binomial situations.

....

Common Core State Standards

7.SP.C.5 Understand that probability of a chance event is a number between 0 and 1 that expresses the likelihood of the event occurring. Large numbers indicate greater likelihood. A probability near 0 indicates an unlikely event, a probability around 1 indicates an event that is neither unlikely nor likely, and a probability near 1 indicates a likely event.

7.SP.C.8.a Understand that, just as with simple events, the probability of a compound event is the fraction of outcomes in the sample space for which the compound event occurs.

7.SP.C.8.b Represent sample spaces for compound events using methods such as organized lists, tables, and tree diagrams. For an event described in everyday language (e.g. "rolling double sixes"), identify the outcomes in the sample space which compose the event.

Also 7.RP.A.2, 7.RP.A.2a, 7.RP.A.3, 7.SP.C.7, 7.SP.C.7a, 7.SP.C.7b, 7.SP.C.8, 7.SP.C.8c

5.1 Guessing Answers
Finding More Expected Values

Have you ever forgotten to study for a true/false quiz? Have you then tried to guess at the answers? If this happens, you might decide to flip a coin and choose Heads = True and Tails = False.

- What is your chance of getting Question 1 correct?

- What are your chances of getting every question correct?

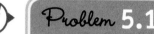

Problem 5.1

A quiz has four true/false questions. Each question is worth 25 points.

Directions

- Write the numbers 1–4 on paper to represent the questions for the quiz.

- Toss a penny to determine the answer for each quiz item.

- Write T *(true)* if a head shows and F *(false)* if a tail shows.

- After you have written your answers, your teacher will give you the correct answer.

- Mark your answers *correct* or *incorrect*. Record your score.

A Compare answers with your classmates. How many papers had

1. exactly 4 correct (all correct)?

2. exactly 3 correct (3 correct and 1 incorrect)?

3. exactly 2 correct (2 correct and 2 incorrect)?

4. exactly 1 correct (1 correct and 3 incorrect)?

5. none correct (0 correct and 4 incorrect)?

6. What is the experimental probability of getting all 4 correct? Exactly 3 correct? Exactly 2 correct? Exactly 1 correct? None correct?

Problem 5.1 continued

B 1. How many different ways can you get all 4 correct? Exactly 3 correct? Exactly 2 correct? Exactly 1 correct? None correct?

2. Find the theoretical probability of each score below.

  a. 100 (all correct)

  b. 75 (exactly three correct)

  c. 50 (exactly two correct)

  d. 25 (exactly one correct)

  e. 0 (all incorrect)

C 1. Suppose you take the quiz 32 times. How many times do you expect to get 4 correct answers? 3 correct answers? 2 correct answers? 1 correct answer? 0 correct answers?

2. What would your total score be in each case?

3. If you take the quiz 32 times, what is the expected average score? Will the expected value change if you take the quiz 100 times? Explain.

D Suppose the true/false quiz has five questions and you guess each one. What is the probability that you will get them all correct? Explain.

ACE Homework starts on page 105.

5.2 Ortonville
Binomial Probability

In this Problem, you will explore another binomial situation that has equally likely outcomes.

- Suppose you know that a family with five children is moving in next door. What is the probability that the five children are all boys?

Problem 5.2

Ortonville is a very special town. Each family is named Orton and has exactly five children. Below are the names given to the Ortonville children.

The Orton Children

	Girl	Boy
First-Born Child	Gloria	Benson
Second-Born Child	Gilda	Berndt
Third-Born Child	Gail	Blair
Fourth-Born Child	Gerri	Blake
Fifth-Born Child	Gina	Brett

A List all of the possible outcomes for a family with five children.

B What is the probability that a family has children named Gloria, Gilda, Blair, Blake, and Gina?

C Find the probability that a family has

1. exactly five girls or five boys.

2. two girls and three boys.

3. the first or last child a boy.

4. at least one boy.

5. at most one boy.

ACE Homework starts on page 105.

5.3 A Baseball Series
Expanding Binomial Probability

Every fall the best baseball team in the American League plays the best team in the National League. The series has up to seven games. The first team to win four games wins the series.

Suppose the Bobcats are playing the Gazelles in a youth baseball championship 7-game series. The teams enter the series evenly matched. That is, they each have an equally likely chance of winning each game.

The Gazelles have won the first two games of the series.

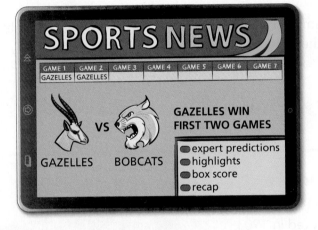

- What is a likely ending for this series?

Let us consider *all* of the possible outcomes for the last 5 games.

Label the outcomes with a G for a Gazelles win or a B for a Bobcats win. For example, BBGG means that, after the Gazelles won the first two games, the Bobcats win the third and fourth games, and the Gazelles win the fifth and sixth games. In this example, the series ends in six games (6), when the Gazelles have won four games (G). In baseball notation, this is written G-6.

- What does BBBGG mean? Who won the series?

- What does BBBB mean? Do they need to play a seventh game?

- What does BBGB mean? Who is more likely to win this series?

> **?**
> - What is the probability that the series will end in 4 games? 5 games? 6 games? 7 games?
> - What is the probability that the Bobcats win the series?

Problem 5.3

A Before you analyze the rest of the series, predict whether it is more probable that the series will end in 4, 5, 6, or 7 games.

B Suppose all five remaining games are played. What are all of the possible outcomes for these five games? Include all possibilities even if there is a winner before all seven games are played.

C **1.** For each outcome, determine the length of the series.

2. What is the probability that the series ends in four games? In five games? In six games? In seven games?

D Analyze the outcomes in Question C for wins. What is the probability that the Gazelles win the series? That the Bobcats with the series?

A C E Homework starts on page 105.

Did You Know?

The World Series started in 1903 as a best-of-nine-game series. From 1905 until 1919, the series changed to the best-of-seven games.

After World War I ended, the series temporarily changed back to the best-of-nine games in 1919 to 1921. From 1922 until now, the series has remained a best-of-seven series.

Between 1922 and 2012 the World Series ended in four games nineteen times. It ended in five games eighteen times. It ended in six games eighteen times and in seven games thirty-five times. There was no World Series in 1994.

Applications

1. It costs six tickets to play the Toss-a-Penny game at the school carnival. For each turn, a player tosses a penny three times. If the penny lands heads up two or more times in a turn, the player wins ten tickets to spend on food and games.

   a. Suppose Benito plays the game 80 times. How many tickets can he expect to win?

   b. What is the average number of tickets Benito can expect to win or to lose per turn?

2. **a.** Suppose you toss three coins at the same time. Your friend tosses one coin three times in a row.

   Is the probability of your getting three heads the *same as* or *different from* your friend's? Explain your reasoning.

   b. Suppose you toss three coins and get three tails. What is the probability you will get three tails the next time you toss the three coins? Explain.

   c. Is the probability of getting three heads in three tosses the same, greater, or less than the probability of getting three tails in three tosses?

   d. Is the probability of getting two heads in three tosses the same, greater, or less than the probability of getting one head in three tosses?

For Exercises 3–9, use this information: Scout, Ms. Rodriguez's dog, is about to have puppies. The vet thinks Scout will have four puppies. Assume that for each puppy, a male and female are equally likely.

3. **a.** List all of the possible combinations of female and male puppies that Scout might have.

   b. Is Scout more likely to have four male puppies or two male and two female puppies? Explain.

4. **Multiple Choice** What is the probability that Scout will have four female puppies?

   A. $\frac{1}{2}$ **B.** $\frac{1}{4}$ **C.** $\frac{1}{8}$ **D.** $\frac{1}{16}$

5. **Multiple Choice** What is the probability that Scout will have two male and two female puppies?

   F. $\frac{1}{4}$ **G.** $\frac{3}{4}$ **H.** $\frac{1}{8}$ **J.** $\frac{3}{8}$

6. **Multiple Choice** What is the probability that Scout will have at least one male puppy?

   A. $\frac{15}{16}$ **B.** $\frac{7}{8}$ **C.** $\frac{3}{4}$ **D.** $\frac{1}{2}$

7. **Multiple Choice** What is the probability that Scout will have at least one female puppy?

   F. $\frac{15}{16}$ **G.** $\frac{7}{8}$ **H.** $\frac{3}{4}$ **J.** $\frac{1}{2}$

8. Ms. Rodriguez plans to sell her dog's female puppies for $250 each and her male puppies for $200 each. How much money can she expect to make from a litter of four puppies?

9. Suppose the vet thinks Scout will have a litter of five puppies. How much money can Ms. Rodriguez expect to make from selling the puppies?

10. Rajan's physical education class divides into two teams. The two teams are evenly matched. One team is the Champs, and the other team is the Stars. The series is five games. The first team to win three games wins the series. The Champs win the first game.

    a. What is the probability that the series will end in 3, 4, or 5 games?

    b. What is the probability that the Stars will win the series?

Connections

11. You might find that a tree diagram is a helpful model in this Exercise.

   a. List the possible outcomes when you toss a coin three times.

   b. How many outcomes are there when you toss a coin four times? (You do not have to list them all.) Five times?

   c. How many ways can you get five heads in five tosses? How many ways can you get zero heads in five tosses? How many ways can you get four heads? Three heads? Two heads? One head?

   d. Explain why some symmetry in your answers in part (c) makes sense.

12. The largest hamster litter on record consisted of 26 babies. Suppose a hamster has 26 babies. Assume that for each baby, females and males are equally likely. What is the theoretical probability that all 26 babies will be male? Explain your reasoning.

13. Drew walks her neighbors' dogs. She collects $10 per week from each neighbor. One neighbor offers her these deals.

   a. Toss five coins. If there are four or more heads, the customer pays $18. Otherwise, he pays $4. Find the expected value for this deal. Decide if it is a fair deal.

   b. Toss five coins. If they are all the same, the customer pays $80. Otherwise, he pays $4. Find the expected value for this deal. Decide if it is a fair deal.

14. King George's home, Castle Warwick, is under siege. King George must escape to Castle Howard. The only escape route is through a series of canals, shown below.

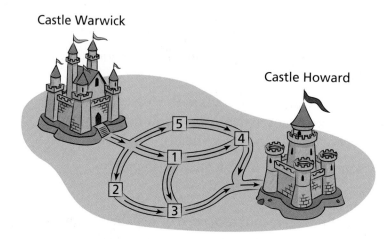

Castle Warwick

Castle Howard

There are five gates in the series of canals. Each gate opens and closes at random and is open half the time and closed the other half. The arrows show the way the water is flowing.

a. What is the probability that a water route from Castle Warwick to Castle Howard is open?

b. How is this problem similar to Problem 5.3?

15. Ethan makes a game played on the number line.

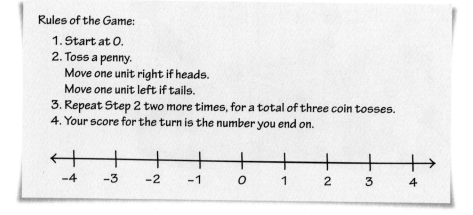

Rules of the Game:
1. Start at 0.
2. Toss a penny.
   Move one unit right if heads.
   Move one unit left if tails.
3. Repeat Step 2 two more times, for a total of three coin tosses.
4. Your score for the turn is the number you end on.

a. What scores are possible after one turn (three tosses)?

b. Suppose Ethan changes his game so that a turn consists of four tosses. What scores are possible after one turn?

16. a. For the spinner below, what are the possible outcomes of a single spin? What is the probability of each outcome?

b. Spinning the spinner from part (a) three times is also a binomial situation. What is the probability of RBB (in this order)?

c. Using this spinner below once is not a binomial situation. What are the possible outcomes? What is the probability of each?

d. Does spinning the spinner below make a binomial situation? Explain your reasoning.

e. Suppose you spin the spinner in part (d) three times. What is the probability of RBB (in this order)?

Extensions

Pascal's Triangle (on the left, below) can be used to summarize binomial probabilities and answer new questions in some binomial situations. The sum of each row is the same as the number of outcomes in a binomial probability. For example, some binomial situations are written across from their corresponding row.

Pascal's Triangle	Coin	True/False Test
1	Tossing 1 coin	1 question
1 1	Tossing 2 coins	2 questions
1 2 1	Tossing 3 coins	3 questions
1 3 3 1	Tossing 4 coins	4 questions
1 4 6 4 1	Tossing 5 coins	5 questions
1 5 10 10 5 1		

For Exercises 17 and 18, use Pascal's Triangle above.

17. Describe some patterns in Pascal's Triangle.

18. What is the sixth row (the next row in the diagram above) of Pascal's Triangle? Describe what probabilities each number represents in a situation that involves tossing 6 coins.

For Exercises 19–21, tell which row from Pascal's Triangle you used.

19. On a five-question true/false test, what is the probability that you will guess exactly two correct answers?

20. A coin is tossed six times. What is the probability that at least two heads occur?

21. On a nine-question true/false test, what is the probability that you will guess exactly three correct answers?

Mathematical Reflections 5

In this Investigation, you looked at probabilities for situations involving a series of actions, each with two equally likely outcomes. The following questions will help you summarize what you have learned.

Think about these questions. Discuss your ideas with other students and your teacher. Then write a summary of your findings in your notebook.

1. **Describe** five different binomial situations. **Explain** why they are binomial situations.

2. Tossing a coin three times is an example of a situation involving a series of three actions, each with two equally likely outcomes.

   a. **Pick** one of the situations in Question 1. **Describe** a series of three actions, each with two equally likely outcomes. Make a list of all the possible outcomes.

   b. **Write** a question about your situation that can be answered by your list.

3. As you increase the number of actions for a binomial situation, what happens to the total number of possible outcomes? For example, suppose you increase the number of times a coin is tossed. **What** happens to the total number of outcomes?

Common Core Mathematical Practices

As you worked on the Problems in this Investigation, you used prior knowledge to make sense of them. You also applied Mathematical Practices to solve the Problems. Think back over your work, the ways you thought about the Problems, and how you used Mathematical Practices.

Tori described her thoughts in the following way:

> We analyzed a baseball series in Problem 5.3. We had to predict which number of games was likely to end the series. We guessed 5 games.
>
> We determined the different options for how the series could play out. Then, we looked at different ways each team could win the series.
>
> Then, we listed all of the options and found the actual probabilities for ending in 4, 5, 6, or 7 games. We had to use strategies similar to the ones we used in the Problems 5.1 and 5.2.
>
> ....
>
> **Common Core Standards for Mathematical Practice**
>
> **MP1** Make sense of problems and persevere in solving them

- What other Mathematical Practices can you identify in Tori's reasoning?

- Describe a Mathematical Practice that you and your classmates used to solve a different Problem in this Investigation.

Unit Project

The Carnival Game

This Project requires you to use the mathematics you have studied in several Units, including this one. You will make a game for a school carnival and test your game. Then, you will write a report to the carnival committee about your game.

Part 1: Design a Carnival Game

You can design a new game or redesign one of the games you analyzed in this Unit. Keep these guidelines in mind.

- The game should make a profit for the school.
- The game should be easy to set up and use at a school carnival. It should not require expensive equipment.
- The game should take a relatively short time to play.
- Your friends and peers should easily understand the rules of the game.

Part 2: Test Your Game

After you have drafted a game design, you will need to try out your game. You should play the game several times until you feel confident that you can predict what will happen in the long run. Keep track of your trials and include that information in your report.

Part 3: Submit Your Game Design to the Carnival Committee

Once you are satisfied that your game is reasonable, prepare to submit your design. Your submission to the committee should include two things: a model or a scale model of the game and a written report.

Model or Scale Model

If you build a scale model instead of an actual model, give the scale factor from the scale model to the actual game.

You can either construct the model out of materials similar to those you would use for the actual game, or you can prepare scale drawings of the game. If you make drawings, be sure to include enough views of your game so that anyone could look at the drawings and construct the game.

Rules

Include a set of rules with your model that explains how the game is played, how much it costs to play, how a player wins, and the value of what a player wins.

Part 4: Write a Report

Write a report about your game to the carnival committee. Assume that the committee consists of teachers in the building (not just mathematics teachers), parents, and other students. Your report should include:

- The experimental probability of winning the game you found from playing the game several times

- The theoretical probability of winning the game, if possible

- An explanation of why you were unable to calculate the theoretical probability, if unable to find it

- The amount of money the school will collect and how much they should expect to pay out if the game is played many times

- Explanations for how you determined the amounts of money collected and paid out

- An explanation of why your game should be chosen, why the game is worth having in the carnival, and why you think people would want to play it

Looking Back

In this Unit, you studied some basic ideas of probability and some ways to use those ideas to solve problems about probability and expected value. In particular, you studied how to

- Find and interpret experimental and theoretical probabilities

- Use simulations to gather experimental data

- Use tree diagrams and other listing techniques to find all of the possible outcomes

- Use area models in which probabilities are shown as parts of a whole square

Use Your Understanding: Probability Reasoning

To test your understanding and skill with probability ideas and strategies, consider the following problem situations.

1. Maria's homework problem is to design two dartboards that match these conditions:
   - The probability of landing in region A is 30%.
   - The probability of landing in region B is 25%.
   - The probability of landing in region C is 20%.
   - The remaining space on the dartboard is region D.

   a. Draw a square dartboard that meets the given conditions.
   b. Find the probability that a dart will land in region D.
   c. Find the probability that a dart will land in a region other than D.
   d. Find the probability that a dart will *not* land in region A.

2. Gabrielle and Nick are playing the Match/No Match game. On each turn, the players spin the two spinners shown below. Gabrielle scores 1 point if the spins match, and Nick scores 1 point if they do not match.

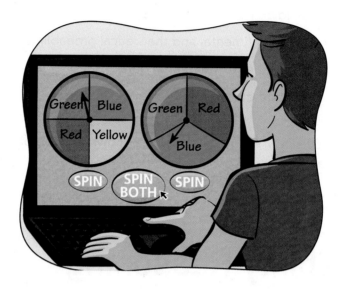

a. Use a tree diagram to show all of the possible outcomes for this game.

b. What is the theoretical probability of getting a match?

c. What is the theoretical probability of getting a nonmatch?

d. Does each player have an equally likely chance of winning? Explain your reasoning.

e. Is this a fair game? If so, explain why. If not, explain how you could change the rules to make it fair.

3. Kali designed a new computer game. She programmed the game so the probability that a player will win is $\frac{1}{4}$ on each turn. If the player wins, the score increases by four points. If the player loses, two points are deducted from the score.

a. Matthew plans to play 12 rounds of the game. How many points can he expect to score?

b. How many points per round can Matthew expect to win or lose?

c. Is this a fair game? If not, how would you change the points won or lost so that it is a fair game?

Explain Your Reasoning

When you use mathematical calculations or diagrams to solve a problem or make a decision, it is important to justify your reasoning. Answer these questions about your work.

4. What does it mean to say that the probability of an event is $\frac{1}{2}$, $\frac{2}{3}$, or $\frac{5}{8}$?

5. How are experimental and theoretical probabilities of an event related to each other?

6. What does it mean when a set of outcomes is *not* equally likely?

7. Explain and illustrate with a specific example how you could use each strategy to analyze probabilities.

   a. tree diagrams

   b. area models

8. What does it mean to find the expected value of a chance activity with numerical outcomes? Give three examples of Problems in this Unit for which you had to find the expected value.

English / Spanish Glossary

A **area model** A diagram in which fractions of the area of the diagram correspond to probabilities in a situation. For example, suppose there are three blue blocks and two red blocks in a container. If one block is drawn out at a time, and the block drawn each time is replaced, the area model below shows that the probability of getting two red blocks is $\frac{4}{25}$.

Area models are particularly helpful when the outcomes being analyzed are not equally likely, because more likely outcomes take up larger areas. Area models are also helpful for outcomes involving more than one stage, such as rolling a number cube and then tossing a coin.

modelo de área Un diagrama en el que las fracciones del área del diagrama corresponden a las probabilidades de una situación. Por ejemplo, supón que hay tres bloques azules y dos bloques rojos en un recipiente. Si se saca un bloque a la vez, reemplazando el bloque que se saca cada vez, el modelo de área de abajo muestra que la probabilidad de sacar dos bloques rojos es $\frac{4}{25}$.

Los modelos de área son especialmente útiles cuando los resultados que se analizan no son igualmente probables, porque los resultados más probables ocupan áreas más grandes. Los modelos de área son también útiles para resultados que incluyen más de un paso, como lanzar un cubo numérico y luego lanzar una moneda al aire.

Second Choice

		B	B	B	R	R
	B	BB	BB	BB	BR	BR
	B	BB	BB	BB	BR	BR
First Choice	B	BB	BB	BB	BR	BR
	R	RB	RB	RB	RR	RR
	R	RB	RB	RB	RR	RR

B **binomial probability** The probability of getting one of two possible outcomes over many trials. For example, the probability of getting a heads or tails when tossing a coin or the probability of getting a 5 or not 5 when rolling a number cube.

probabilidad del binomio La probabilidad de obtener uno de dos resultados posibles en varias pruebas. Por ejemplo, la probabilidad de obtener cara o cruz cuando se lanza una moneda al aire o la probabilidad de obtener o no un 5 cuando se lanza un cubo numérico.

C **compound event** An event that consists of two or more simple events. For example, tossing a coin is a simple event. Tossing two coins, and examining combinations of outcomes, is a compound event.

evento compuesto Evento que consiste de dos o más eventos simples. Por ejemplo, lanzar una moneda al aire es un evento simple. Lanzar dos monedas al aire y examinar combinaciones de resultados, es un evento compuesto.

D describe Academic Vocabulary To explain or tell in detail. A written description can contain facts and other information needed to communicate an answer. A diagram or a graph may also be included.

related terms *explain, present*

sample Three of ten rolls of a number cube result in a 5. Describe the theoretical and experimental probability of rolling a 5.

describir Vocabulario académico Explicar o decir con detalle. Una descripción escrita puede contener datos y otra información necesaria para comunicar una respuesta. También se puede incluir un diagrama o una gráfica.

términos relacionados *explicar, presentar*

ejemplo En tres de diez lanzamientos de un cubo numérico obtienes un 5. Describe la probabilidad teórica y experimental de obtener un 5.

Since a number cube has six identical sides and the number 5 appears once, the theoretical probability of rolling a 5 is $\frac{1}{6}$. The experimental probability of rolling a 5 is $\frac{3}{10}$.

Como un cubo numérico tiene seis caras iguales y el número 5 aparece una sola vez, la probabilidad teórica de que salga un 5 es $\frac{1}{6}$. La probabilidad experimental de que salga un 5 es $\frac{3}{10}$.

design Academic Vocabulary To make using specific criteria.

related terms *draw, plan, outline, model*

sample A computer game randomly hides a treasure chest. The probability that the treasure chest will be hidden in the sand is 50%, in the water 30%, in the rocks 10%, or in the grass 10%. Design a computer screen for this game.

diseñar Vocabulario académico Crear algo usando criterios específicos.

términos relacionados *dibujar, planear, bosquejar, representar*

ejemplo Un juego de computadora oculta al azar un cofre del tesoro. La probabilidad de que el cofre del tesoro esté escondido en la arena es de 50%, en el agua de 30%, en las rocas de 10% o en el pasto de 10%. Diseña una pantalla de computadora para este juego.

I'll draw 50 of the 100 square units as sand, 30 as water, and 10 each as rocks and grass to match each probability.

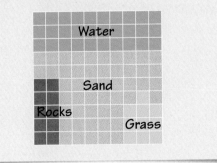

Dibujaré 50 de los 100 cuadrados unitarios para la arena, 30 para el agua, 10 para las rocas y 10 para el pasto, para representar cada probabilidad.

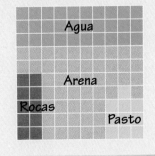

determine Academic Vocabulary To use the given information and any related facts to find a value or make a decision.

related terms *solve, evaluate, examine*

sample Eugene's favorite shirts are red, black, orange, and white. His favorite hats are red, gold, and black. Eugene randomly selects one shirt and one hat. Make a chart to determine the probability that they are the same color.

determinar Vocabulario académico Usar la información dada y cualquier dato relacionado para hallar un valor o tomar una decisión.

términos relacionados *resolver, evaluar, examinar*

ejemplo Las camisetas favoritas de Eugene son rojas, negras, anaranjadas y blancas. Sus gorras favoritas son rojas, doradas y negras. Eugene selecciona al azar una camiseta y una gorra. Haz una gráfica para determinar la probabilidad de que sean del mismo color.

The chart shows 12 possible combinations. The probability of the same color is $\frac{2}{12}$, or $\frac{1}{6}$.

Hats

	R	G	B
R	RR	RG	RB
B	BR	BG	BB
O	OR	OG	OB
W	WR	WG	WB

Shirts

La tabla muestra 12 combinaciones posibles. La probabilidad de que sean del mismo color es de $\frac{2}{12}$ ó $\frac{1}{6}$.

Gorras

	R	D	N
R	RR	RD	RN
N	NR	ND	NN
A	AR	AD	AN
B	BR	BD	BN

Camisetas

E **equally likely** Two or more events that have the same probability of occurring. For example, when you toss a fair coin, heads and tails are equally likely; each has a 50% chance of happening. Rolling a six-sided number cube gives a $\frac{1}{6}$ probability for each number to come up. Each outcome is equally likely.

igualmente probables Dos o más eventos que tienen la misma probabilidad de ocurrir. Por ejemplo, cuando lanzas una moneda al aire, la probabilidad de obtener cara es igual a la de obtener cruz; es decir, cada caso tiene una probabilidad del 50% de ocurrir. Lanzar un cubo numérico de 6 lados supone $\frac{1}{6}$ de probabilidad de que salga cada número. Cada resultado es igualmente probable.

expected value (or long-term average) Intuitively, the average payoff over the long run. For example, suppose you are playing a game with two number cubes. You score 2 points when a sum of 6 is rolled, 1 point for a sum of 3, and 0 points for anything else. If you roll the cubes 36 times, you could expect to roll a sum of 6 five times, a sum of 3 twice, and the other sums 29 times. This means that you could expect to score $(5 \times 2) + (2 \times 1) + (29 \times 0) = 12$ points for 36 rolls, an average of $\frac{12}{36} = \frac{1}{3}$ point per roll. Here, $\frac{1}{3}$ is the expected value, or long-term average, of one roll.

valor esperado (o promedio a largo plazo) El promedio de puntos o recompensas que se espera obtener a largo plazo. Por ejemplo, imagínate un juego con dos cubos numéricos en el que obtienes 2 puntos por una suma de 6, 1 punto por una suma de 3 y 0 puntos por cualquier otra suma. Si lanzas los cubos numéricos 36 veces, puedes esperar obtener una suma de 6 cinco veces, una suma de 3 dos veces, y las otras sumas 29 veces. Esto significa que puedes esperar conseguir $(5 \times 2) + (2 \times 1) + (29 \times 0) = 12$ puntos por 36 lanzamientos, o sea un promedio de $\frac{12}{36} = \frac{1}{3}$ de punto por lanzamiento. Aquí $\frac{1}{3}$ es el valor esperado, o promedio a largo plazo, de un lanzamiento.

experimental probability A probability that is determined through experimentation. For example, you could find the experimental probability of getting a head when you toss a coin by tossing a coin many times and keeping track of the outcomes. The experimental probability would be the ratio of the number of heads to the total number of tosses, or trials. Experimental probability may not be the same as the theoretical probability. However, for a large number of trials, they are likely to be close. Experimental probabilities are used to predict behavior over the long run.

probabilidad experimental La probabilidad que se determina mediante la experimentación. Por ejemplo, puedes hallar la probabilidad experimental de obtener cara cuando lanzas una moneda al aire al efectuar numerosos tiros y llevar la cuenta de los resultados. La probabilidad experimental sería la razón del número de caras al número total de tiros o pruebas. La probabilidad experimental puede no ser igual a la probabilidad teórica. Sin embargo, en un gran número de pruebas, es probable que estén cerca. Las probabilidades experimentales se usan para predecir lo que ocurrirá largo plazo.

explain Academic Vocabulary To give facts and details that make an idea easier to understand. Explaining can involve a written summary supported by a diagram, chart, table, or a combination of these.

related terms *clarify, describe, justify*

sample Find the probability of tossing a coin 3 times and getting heads exactly two times. Explain your reasoning.

I can use a tree diagram to look at all eight possible outcomes when tossing a coin three times.

Toss 1	Toss 2	Toss 3	Results
H	H	H	HHH
		T	HHT
	T	H	HTH
		T	HTT
T	H	H	THH
		T	THT
	T	H	TTH
		T	TTT

There are 3 outcomes in which there are exactly two heads. The probability is $\frac{3}{8}$.

explicar Vocabulario académico Dar datos y detalles que hacen que una idea sea más fácil de comprender. Explicar puede incluir un resumen escrito apoyado por un diagrama, una gráfica, una tabla o una combinación de estos.

términos relacionados *aclarar, describir, justificar*

ejemplo Halla la probabilidad de lanzar una moneda al aire tres veces y obtener cara exactamente dos veces. Explica tu razonamiento.

Puedo usar un diagrama arborescente para observar los ocho resultados posibles al lanzar una moneda al aire tres veces.

Tirada 1	Tirada 2	Tirada 3	Resultados
C	C	C	CCC
		Cr	CCCr
	Cr	C	CCrC
		Cr	CCrCr
Cr	C	C	CrCC
		Cr	CrCCr
	Cr	C	CrCrC
		Cr	CrCrCr

Hay 3 resultados en que hay exactamente dos caras. La probabilidad es de $\frac{3}{8}$.

fair game A game in which each player is equally likely to win. The probability of winning a two-person fair game is $\frac{1}{2}$. An unfair game can be made fair by adjusting the scoring system, or the payoffs. For example, suppose you play a game in which two fair coins are tossed. You score when both coins land heads up. Otherwise, your opponent scores. The probability that you will score is $\frac{1}{4}$, and the probability that your opponent will score is $\frac{3}{4}$. To make the game fair, you might adjust the scoring system so that you receive 3 points each time you score and your opponent receives 1 point when he or she scores. This would make the expected values for each player equal, which results in a fair game.

juego justo Un juego en el que cada jugador tiene igual probabilidad de ganar. La probabilidad de ganar en un juego justo entre dos personas es $\frac{1}{2}$. Para hacer justo un juego injusto se puede ajustar el sistema de reparto de puntos o de recompensas. Por ejemplo, imagina un juego que consiste en lanzar dos monedas al aire. Si salen dos caras, tú obtienes puntos. Si no, los obtiene el otro jugador. La probabilidad de que tú obtengas los puntos es $\frac{1}{4}$ y la probabilidad de que los obtenga el otro jugador es $\frac{3}{4}$. Para hacer que el juego sea justo, podrías ajustar el sistema de reparto de puntos de manera que, cada vez que salgan dos caras, tú recibas 3 puntos y en las demás ocasiones el otro jugador reciba 1 punto. Esto haría que los valores esperados para cada jugador fueran iguales, lo que daría como resultado en un juego justo.

favorable outcome An outcome that gives a desired result. A favorable outcome is sometimes called a *success*. For example, when you toss two coins to find the probability of the coins matching, HH and TT are favorable outcomes.

resultado favorable Un resultado que proporciona una consecuencia deseada. A veces, a un resultado favorable se le llama un éxito. Por ejemplo, cuando lanzas dos monedas al aire para hallar la probabilidad de que las dos coincidan, los resultados CC y CrCr son resultados favorables.

L **Law of Large Numbers** This law states, in effect, that as more trials of an experiment are conducted, the experimental probability more closely approximates the theoretical probability. It is not at all unusual to have 100% heads after three tosses of a fair coin, but it would be extremely unusual to have even 60% heads after 1,000 tosses. This is expressed by the Law of Large Numbers.

Ley de números grandes Esta ley establece, en efecto, que a medida que se realicen más pruebas de un experimento, más se acercar· la probabilidad experimental a la probabilidad teórica. No es inusual obtener el 100% de caras después de tres lanzamientos de una moneda justa al aire, pero sería extremadamente inusual obtener incluso el 60% de caras después de 1,000 lanzamientos. Esto se expresa en la ley de los números grandes.

outcome A possible result. For example, when a number cube is rolled, the possible outcomes are 1, 2, 3, 4, 5, and 6. Other possible outcomes are even or odd. Others are three and not three. When determining probabilities, it is important to be clear about what the possible outcomes are.

resultado Una consecuencia posible. Por ejemplo, cuando se lanza un cubo numérico, los resultados posibles son 1, 2, 3, 4, 5 y 6. Otros resultados posibles son pares o impares. Incluso otro es tres y no tres. Cuando se determinan las probabilidades, es importante definir cuáles son los resultados posibles.

payoff The number of points (or dollars or other objects of value) a player in a game receives for a particular outcome.

recompensa El número de puntos (o dólares u otros objetos de valor) que recibe un jugador por un resultado particular.

probability A number between 0 and 1 that describes the likelihood that an outcome will occur. For example, when a fair number cube is rolled, a 2 can be expected $\frac{1}{6}$ of the time, so the probability of rolling a 2 is $\frac{1}{6}$. The probability of a certain outcome is 1, while the probability of an impossible outcome is 0.

probabilidad Un número comprendido entre 0 y 1 que describe la probabilidad de que ocurra un resultado. Por ejemplo, cuando se lanza un cubo numérico justo, se puede esperar un 2 cada $\frac{1}{6}$ de las veces, por tanto, probabilidad de obtener un 2 es $\frac{1}{6}$. La probabilidad de un cierto resultado es 1, mientras que la probabilidad de un resultado imposible es 0.

random Outcomes that are uncertain when viewed individually, but which exhibit a predictable pattern over many trials. For example, when you roll a fair number cube, you have no way of knowing what the next roll will be, but you do know that, over the long run, you will roll each number on the cube about the same number of times.

aleatorio(s) Resultados que son inciertos cuando se consideran individualmente, pero que presentan un patrón predecible a lo largo de muchas pruebas. Por ejemplo, cuando lanzas un cubo numérico, es imposible saber cuál será el resultado del siguiente lanzamiento, pero sabes que, a la larga, obtendrás cada uno de los números del cubo numérico aproximadamente el mismo número de veces.

relative frequency The ratio of the number of desired results to the total number of trials.

frecuencia relativa La razón del número de resultados deseados al número total de pruebas.

sample space The set of all possible outcomes in a probability situation. When you toss two coins, the sample space consists of four outcomes: HH, HT, TH, and TT.

espacio muestral El conjunto de todos los resultados posibles en una situación de probabilidad. Cuando lanzas dos monedas al aire, el espacio muestral consiste en cuatro resultados: CC, CCr, CrC y CrCr.

simulation An experiment using objects that represent the relevant characteristics of a real-world situation.

simulación Experimento en el que se usan objetos para representar las características relevantes de una situación de la vida diaria.

theoretical probability A probability obtained by analyzing a situation. If all the outcomes are equally likely, you can find a theoretical probability of an event by listing all the possible outcomes and then finding the ratio of the number of outcomes producing the desired event to the total number of outcomes. For example, there are 36 possible equally likely outcomes (number pairs) when two fair number cubes are rolled. Of these, six have a sum of 7, so the probability of rolling a sum of 7 is $\frac{6}{36}$, or $\frac{1}{6}$. Since the sum of the probabilities of all possible events must be 1, theoretical probability can be applied to events that are not equally likely. The probability of rolling a sum of 7 is $\frac{1}{6}$, and the probability of not rolling a 7 is $\frac{5}{6}$.

probabilidad teórica La probabilidad que se obtiene mediante el an·lisis de una situación. Si todos los resultados son igualmente probables, puedes hallar una probabilidad teórica de un evento haciendo una lista de todos los resultados posibles y luego hallando la razón del número de resultados que produce el evento deseado al número total de resultados. Por ejemplo, al lanzar dos cubos numéricos, hay 36 resultados igualmente probables (pares de números). De estos, seis tienen una suma de 7, por tanto, la probabilidad de obtener una suma de 7 es $\frac{6}{36}$ ó $\frac{1}{6}$. Dado que la suma de las probabilidades de todos los eventos posibles debe ser 1, la probabilidad teórica también se puede aplicar a eventos que no son igualmente probables. La probabilidad de obtener una suma de 7 es $\frac{1}{6}$ y la probabilidad de *no* obtener un 7 es $\frac{5}{6}$.

tree diagram A diagram used to determine the number of possible outcomes in a probability situation. The number of final branches is equal to the number of possible outcomes. The tree diagram below shows all the possible outcomes for randomly choosing a yellow or a red rose and then a white or a pink ribbon. The four possible outcomes are listed in the last column. Tree diagrams are handy to use when outcomes are equally likely.

diagrama de árbol Un diagrama que se usa para determinar el número de resultados posibles en una situación de probabilidad. El número de ramas finales es igual al número de resultados posibles. El siguiente diagrama de árbol muestra todos los resultados posibles de escoger al azar una rosa amarilla o roja, y luego una cinta blanca o rosada. Los cuatro resultados posibles aparecen en la última columna. Los diagramas de árbol son útiles cuando los resultados son igualmente probables.

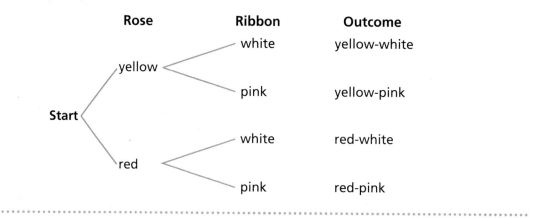

trial One round of an experiment. For example, if you are interested in the behavior of a coin, you might experiment by tossing a coin 50 times and recording the results. Each toss is a trial, so this experiment consists of 50 trials.

prueba Una ronda de un experimento. Por ejemplo, si te interesan los resultados de lanzar una moneda al aire, puedes hacer un experimento lanzando una moneda al aire 50 veces y anotando los resultados. Cada lanzamiento es una prueba, por tanto, este experimento consiste en 50 pruebas.

Index

ACE
  binomial outcomes, 105–110
  chance, 17–24
  compound events and area
    models, 80–96
  decision-making with
    probability, 58–68
  experimental and theoretical
    probability, 36–47

area models, 117, 118
  ACE, 80–96
  compound events and,
    71–72
  finding expected value,
    78–79
  finding the sample space,
    72–74
  Mathematical Reflections,
    97–98
  probability and, 75
  simulations and, 76–77

average. *See* expected value

bar graphs, 21, 23, 64

binomial outcomes
  ACE, 105–110
  binomial probability, 99,
    101–104
  expected value, 100–101
  Mathematical Reflections,
    111–112

binomial probability, 4, 99,
  101–104, 118

Carnival Game project,
  113–114

chance. *See also* probability
  ACE, 17–24
  decision-making and, 7–8
  equally likely, 15–16
  experimental probabilities,
    12–14
  finding probabilities, 8–11
  Mathematical Reflections,
    25–26

coin tosses
  binomial outcomes, 105, 111
  fair games and, 32–33, 38
  finding probabilities, 8–9,
    13–14, 15, 17, 24, 46

**Common Core Mathematical
  Practices,** 5–6, 26, 49, 70,
  98, 112

compound events, 34, 118

**compound events and area
  models,** 71–72
  ACE, 80–96
  finding expected value,
    78–79
  finding the sample space,
    72–74
  Mathematical Reflections,
    97–98
  probability and, 75
  simulations and, 76–77

contests, 57, 68. *See also* games

data sets, 60

deceptive advertising, 66–67

decimals, 44, 62, 65

**decision-making, probabilities
  and,** 4, 7–8
  ACE, 58–68
  analyzing fairness, 52–53
  analyzing games, 54–55
  finding probabilities, 50–51
  Mathematical Reflections,
    69–70
  possibilities and
    probabilities, 47
  simulations and, 56–57

diagrams. *See* area models; tree
  diagrams

dice. *See* number cubes

equally likely, 15–16, 25, 120.
  See also binomial outcomes
  fair games and, 33, 44

finding probabilities, 18–19,
    23, 26, 117
  outcomes and, 28, 116

equivalent fractions, 65

Evens and Odds game, 66

expected value, 3, 4, 121
  binomial outcomes, 100–101
  compound events and area
    models, 78–79, 97, 98
  finding probabilities, 117

**experimental and theoretical
  probability**
  ACE, 36–47
  developing probability
    models, 30–31
  fair games, 32–33
  finding theoretical
    probabilities, 28–29, 34–35
  Mathematical Reflections,
    48–49
  outcomes and, 27–28

experimental probabilities,
  4, 121
  binomial outcomes, 100
  compound events and area
    models, 76–77, 83
  decision-making with
    probability, 51, 69
  finding, 12–14, 22, 25, 26, 67
  games and, 114
  outcomes and, 48
  predictions and, 37
  simulations and, 57
  theoretical probabilities and,
    29, 35, 37, 117

fair games, 4, 48, 123
  binomial outcomes, 107
  compound events and area
    models, 83
  equally likely and, 15
  Evens and Odds game, 66
  finding probabilities, 43–44

possibilities and probabilities, 32–33
  tree diagrams and, 39

fairness, analyzing, 52–53, 60–61, 69, 70

favorable outcomes, 12, 123

fractions
  binomial outcomes, 106
  decimals and, 44
  developing probability models, 31
  equivalent fractions, 65
  finding probabilities, 9, 11, 12, 20, 22, 45, 61, 62, 63, 117
  number sentences, 41

Galileo, 56

games. *See also* fair games
  coin tosses and, 38
  compound events and area models, 75, 80, 87, 89–90
  decision-making with probability, 54–55
  Evens and Odds game, 66
  Roller Derby game, 31, 54–55, 61, 71
  tree diagrams and, 39

Glossary, 118–126

guessing, binomial outcomes and, 100–101

Investigations
  binomial outcomes, 99–104
  chance, 7–16
  compound events and area models, 71–79
  decision-making with probability, 50–57
  experimental and theoretical probability, 27–35

Law of Large Numbers, 123

likelihood. *See* equally likely

line plots, 45

long-term average. *See* expected value

Looking Ahead, 2–3

Looking Back, 115–117

Mathematical Highlights, 4

Mathematical Practices, 5–6

Mathematical Reflections
  binomial outcomes, 111–112
  chance, 25–26
  compound events and area models, 97–98
  decision-making with probability, 69–70
  experimental and theoretical probability, 48–49

mean. *See* expected value

modeling strategies, 30–31

number cubes
  compound events and area models, 90
  decision-making with probability, 61
  developing probability models, 31
  finding probabilities, 7, 8, 16, 20, 63, 65
  Galileo and, 56
  possible outcomes, 65

number lines, 108

number sentences, 41

outcomes, 4, 124
  binomial outcomes, 99–104
  compound events and area models, 71, 72, 80, 82, 83
  experimental and theoretical probability, 27–28, 48
  favorable outcomes, 12, 123
  finding probabilities and, 38
  possible outcomes, 65
  tree diagrams and, 39, 40

Pascal's Triangle, 110

payoffs, 124

percentages
  compound events and area models, 91, 92

finding probabilities, 9, 11, 12, 20, 22, 36, 62, 63, 64

possibilities and probabilities
  binomial outcomes, 103–104
  fair games and, 32–33
  finding probabilities, 42
  tree diagrams and, 40, 47

possible outcomes, 65

predictions, experimental probabilities and, 37

probabilities. *See also*
  experimental probabilities; possibilities and probabilities; theoretical probabilities
  area models and, 75
  finding, 3, 4, 8–11, 17–18, 115, 124

probability models, 30–31

randomness, 28, 30–31, 45, 124

reasoning, explaining your
  binomial outcomes, 112
  Carnival Game project, 114
  compound events and area models, 82, 98
  decision-making with probability, 70
  equally likely and, 16
  experimental and theoretical probability, 14, 26, 41, 49
  finding probabilities, 11, 24, 117
  finding theoretical probabilities, 28, 29, 35

relative frequency, 12, 124

Roller Derby game, 31, 54–55, 61, 71

sample spaces, 32, 33, 48, 72–74, 125

scale factors, 87

simulations, 56–57, 76–77, 97, 125

spinners
  binomial outcomes, 109
  compound events and area
    models, 75, 77, 82, 89,
    91, 93
  decision-making with
    probability, 58–60
  designing, 68
  finding probabilities,
    50–51, 63

sums, 36, 41

theoretical probabilities, 4, 125

  binomial outcomes, 101, 107
  compound events and area
    models, 77, 80, 82, 83, 84

  decision-making with
    probability, 51, 69
  experimental probabilities
    and, 46, 117
  finding, 28–29, 34–35, 36
  games and, 114
  outcomes and, 48, 116

three-dimensional shapes, 65

tree diagrams, 4, 126
  binomial outcomes, 107
  compound events and area
    models, 81
  fair games and, 32–33

  finding probabilities, 39, 117
  Galileo and, 56
  possible outcomes, 40, 116

trials, 4, 12, 25, 126

two-stage events. *See*
  compound events and area
  models

Unit Project, 113–114

Use Your Understanding,
  115–116

World Series, 104

Index

Acknowledgments

Cover Design

Three Communication Design, Chicago

Photographs

Photo locators denoted as follows: Top (T), Center (C), Bottom (B), Left (L), Right (R), Background (Bkgd)

002 Pearson Education; **003** Shaun Wilkinson/Shutterstock; **013** Rsooll/Fotolia; **028** Pearson Education; **036** Brian Hagiwara/BrandX Pictures/Getty Images; **104** Chicago History Museum/Contributor/Getty Images.